Advanced English

C·A·E

Grammar Practice

RICHARD WALTON

Series Editor: SUE O'CONNELL

Nelson

Nelson English Language Teaching
100 Avenue Road
London NW3 3HF

A division of Thomas Nelson and Sons Ltd

An International Thomson Publishing Company

London • Bonn • Boston • Madrid • Melbourne • Mexico
City • New York • Paris • Singapore • Tokyo

© Richard Walton 1994

First Published by Thomas Nelson and Sons Ltd 1994

ISBN 0-17-556750-6

NPN 9 8 7 6 5 4 3 2 1

For Ron and Mary

Acknowledgements

Many thanks to Sue O'Connell for keeping the book
'focused' and staying positive: and to Roberta for
putting up with it all.

**The publishers would like to thank the following
for permission to reproduce copyright material.
They have tried to contact all copyright holders, but
in cases where they may have failed, will be pleased
to make the necessary arrangements at the first
opportunity.**

Texts
The Independent for the letter 'Pick Strawberry Fields for
the heritage beat' (page 14), Jared Diamond for the
extract 'Indo-European languages' from '*The Rise and
Fall of the Third Chimpanzee*' (page 56), Desk Editor
advertisement reproduced by permission of Guild of
Master Craftsmen Publications Ltd. (page 62), extract
from page 170 of '*Read Better, Read Faster*' by Manya
and Eric De Leeuw (Penguin Books, 1965), © Manya
and Eric De Leeuw, 1965, reproduced by permission of
Penguin Books Ltd. (page 96).

Illustrations
Nigel Paige
Anne Burchell

Contents

Unit 1

1.1 Reduced relative clauses

Decide which of the following sentences contain reduced relative clauses and which do not. Put a tick (✓) in the appropriate column as in the example.

	YES	NO
1 The man called Max at the office and asked him to meet him later that day.		✓
2 The man called Max in the film was played by Patrick Swayze.		
3 Plums used to make me sick when I was a boy.		
4 The player hurt in the tackle had to be taken to hospital.		
5 Coffee made with this new percolator tastes better than ever!		
6 The shark attacked in the shallows, causing panic among the bathers.		
7 The player hurt his knee in the tackle but played on.		
8 Coffee made Brenda feel agitated so she gave up drinking it.		
9 The shark attacked in the shallows swam away losing a lot of blood.		
10 Plums used to make jam must be very ripe.		

1.2 Fill in the gaps

Complete the following sentences with a suitable reduced relative clause and any necessary prepositions. Each sentence must have a passive meaning. Look at the example given.

1 Children *born on* or before 1st September should have been vaccinated.

2 Any books *brought back* to the library more than three days late will be subject to a fine.

3 Meat *~~fried in~~* cooked oil or butter contains much more cholesterol than meat which has been grilled.

4 Patients *given* the new wonder drug showed no greater signs of recovery than those receiving traditional medicine.

5 Did you know that grapes *left* to dry in the sun turn into raisins?

6 Tickets *booked by* phone must be paid for within 24 hours.

7 The management declines all responsibility for property *stolen* from cars *left* this car park.

8 The skeleton *found* the building site last month turned out to be over 2,000 years old.

9 Yes folks, it's true. Clothes *washed in* new 'Spumo' won't lose their colour. We guarantee it!

10 Looking round a junk shop one day, Stanley came across a
   picture ..*painted*......... by Rembrandt.
11 Dogs ..*brought into*.. Britain from another European country must
   spend three months in quarantine.
12 Baggage ......*left*........ unattended may be destroyed.

2 Prepositions

Complete these sentences with a preposition and the appropriate form of a
word taken from the bubble below. Look at the example given.

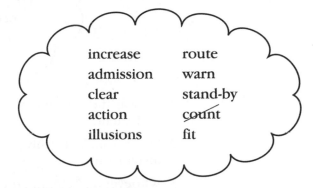

increase   route
admission   warn
clear   stand-by
action   ~~count~~
illusions   fit

1 Dan's rather mean. He thinks a box of chocolates *counts as* a generous
   wedding present!
2 In rough weather the coast guard is ....*on*.... constant ..*Stand-by*..... to
   respond quickly to distress signals from boats.
3 A local woman ....*warned*....... us ...*about*... swimming in the bay. She said
   sharks had been seen there recently.
4 Most people regarded his refusal to answer the question as an ...*admission*...
   ....*of*..... his guilt.
5 The workers were rather cynical after the meeting. Most of them were
   under........ no ..*illusions*..that the management would take their complaints
   seriously.
6 Before applying the solution, make sure the surface to be treated has
   been ..~~clear~~.. ......*of*..... all loose rust and paint.
   cleared
7 The police moved swiftly ....*into*..... ..*action*.... to stop fighting between
   the rival groups of football fans.
8 There has been a dramatic *increase*........ *in*.... the number of cases of
   skin cancer due to damage to the ozone layer.
9 Everyone was confused by the change of timetables and bus
   numbers .....*on*..... this ...*route*...
10 The new model is .....*fitted*... ....*with*.. electric windows, a sun-roof and
   a catalytic converter as standard.

CATALYTIC
CONVERTER
AS STANDARD

3 Irregular verbs

Complete the following sentences by using a suitable tense of the base forms of the verbs in the bubble below. The first one is shown as an example.

spread   sting
grind   hide   strike
lay   ~~bend~~   deal   ride
rise   wind   shrink
dig   bite   freeze
show

1 He was the sort of man who never actually broke the rules but often *bent* them!

2 I always make freshly ...*ground*... coffee for breakfast. I can't stand that instant stuff.

3 Whoever .....~~set~~ *laid*....... the table forgot to put out the fish knives.

4 What's the matter? I've just...~~bitent~~ *bitten*..... my tongue and it really hurts.

5 Unfortunately, the office which ...*deals*.... with lost property was closed for lunch.

6 Apparently, BP has ...*struck*.... oil somewhere in Scandinavia.

7 Don't worry if you can't get any fresh peas, we've got some ..*frozen*... ones in the fridge.

8 Have you ever...*ridden*..a camel? Yes, in Tunisia. I fell off!

9 The hole they ....*dug*.... for the gas pipes was in the wrong place.

10 The watch stopped because you over ...*wound*... it and broke the spring.

11 When I was a child, I was once ...*stung*... in the eye by a bee.

12 OK, come on! Where have you ...*hidden*..my present? It's after midnight so it's my birthday now.

13 That cut looks rather nasty. Have you ...*shown*.. it to the doctor?

14 I'd like to know who it was that ..*spread*..that vicious rumour about Stuart being an ex-convict.

15 The price of petrol ....*rose*...... again last month. It's now twelve per cent more expensive than a year ago.

16 I'm afraid you won't be able to wear your favourite pullover anymore – it's ...*shrunk*.. in the wash!

STUDY TIP ▶   **Irregular verbs**

• A good way of remembering irregular verbs is to record them in groups with similar sounding pasts and past participles:

e.g.	lead	led	led	find	found	found
	say	said	said	wind	wound	wound
	read	read	read	grind	ground	ground

4 Spelling – that can't be right!

In the following sentences some of the underlined verbs are spelt incorrectly. Correct any mistakes, as in the example.

1 I've got a terrible memory, I keep <u>forgetting</u> that girl's name. *t*

2 I think the best sport for all-round fitness must be <u>swiming</u>. *m*

3 I wish you'd stop <u>biting</u> your nails – it's a really unpleasant habit!

4 Come on, let's go to the pub, I'm <u>dieing</u> for a drink! *dying*

5 I see the police have arrested those men who are supposed to have <u>kidnaped</u> that little boy.

6 The crash is a complete mystery. It <u>occurred</u> on a sunny afternoon, with excellent visibility and practically no wind.

7 Louise must have left her credit card behind when she <u>payed</u> for the petrol. *paid*

8 They <u>tryed</u> not to laugh at his accent but just couldn't help it. *tried*

9 Jim and Fay don't seem to be getting on very well these days, they're always <u>argueing</u> about something.

10 Excuse me, Professor. Could you repeat the name of that German scientist you <u>refered</u> to earlier?

11 When I was a boy, I <u>plaied</u> rugby not football. *played*

12 Although the fire was very small, everyone <u>paniced</u> and rushed out of the cinema, causing complete chaos. *k*

STUDY TIP ▶ **Doubling consonants**

- Remember that in verbs of more than one syllable the final consonant is (usually) doubled only if the stress is on the syllable before it:

e.g.   referred   but   offered

              forgetting   remembering

---

5 Formal letters

Fred Smith is writing a letter to Mr Clough, the Chairman of the town council in Loxley. The information in his letter (on page **8**) is correct but the style is far too informal. Rewrite the letter in a more formal style and include the phrases in the bubble below.

I am writing to express
my concern about …

I must insist that you …

I must urge you to …

10 North Parade
Loxley

Dear Mr Clough,

I'm writing to say just how fed up I am with the state of the road outside my house. It's a real mess! Just the other day old Mrs Bicknell, the woman who lives next door, got the back wheel of her Mini stuck in one of the huge great pot-holes outside my gate. The poor old thing was really upset and we had to get two chaps from the garage to pull her car out!

Now why have we got these pot-holes in the road? Well, because of that terrible weather we had with all that ice and snow. But that was two months ago now, and I know you know about the situation because we saw a chap from the council inspecting the road just after the weather got better.

So, why haven't you done anything about it? I think you'd better send a road repair team round here as soon as possible. Not only that, I think it would be a good idea for you to be better prepared in the future so you can get things sorted out a bit more quickly!

Hoping to hear from you very soon about this problem.

Fred Smith

6.1 Wordcheck – Weather and associated hazards

Complete this crossword. One has been done for you.

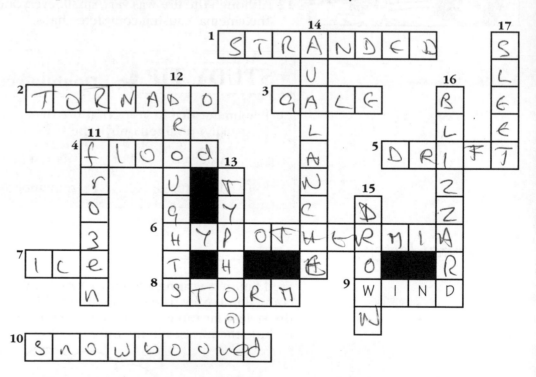

Across

1 If severe weather or a transport problem prevents you from leaving a place, you are .... (8)

2 Violent form of **8 across** with strong circular **9 across**. (7)

3 Very strong **9 across**. (4)

4 A great amount of water in a place that is usually dry. (5)

    5 A pile of snow blown up by **9 across**. (5)

    6 Medical term for when your body temperature falls to a dangerously low level. (11)

    7 Water at 0˚C. (3)

    8 Bad weather with a lot of rain. (5)

    9 A current of air moving across the earth's surface. (4)

10 Blocked in by heavy snow. (9)

Down

11 Having become hard or stiff from cold. (6)

12 Periods of dry weather causing suffering and hardship. (8)

13 A violent hurricane that occurs in the western Pacific. (7)

14 A large mass of snow that slides down the side of a mountain. (9)

15 To die under water because you can't breathe. (5)

16 Heavy snowfall with extremely strong **9 across**. (8)

17 A mixture of rain and snow. (5)

6.2 *Word partners*

Match each word in column **A** with its partner in column **B**. Look at the example.

A		**B**
1 high	E	**A** situation
2 gusty	☐	**B** range
3 torrential	☐	**C** warning
4 severe	☐	**D** level
5 slight	☐	**E** tides
6 desperate	☐	**F** weather
7 gale	☐	**G** seas
8 choppy	☐	**H** rain
9 temperature	☐	**I** winds
10 sea	☐	**J** breeze

Unit 2

1.1 Relative pronouns

Where possible, remove the relative pronouns in the following sentences and make any other necessary changes. Look at the example given.

1 Who's that man that Lisa's talking to?

2 I'm calling about the advert that appeared in yesterday's 'Evening Echo'.

3 Isn't that the hotel where Greg and Sally had their wedding reception?

4 The gentleman with whom you spoke last time is no longer with the company.

5 That's the couple whose house was burgled last week.

6 The bulldog that attacked that little girl has been destroyed.

7 The reason why the accident happened has never been clarified.

8 Is this the picture to which you were referring?

9 She always chooses a moment to call when everyone's out of the office.

10 That's the car that we were thinking of buying.

1.2 Different endings

Each of the sentences below can end in several different ways. Choose the possible endings from the bubble on page **11** and add a suitable relative pronoun where necessary. The first one is shown as an example.

1 What's the name of that town

   a ____which___ was featured in that TV documentary last week?

   b _____ .... ?

   c _____ .... ?

   d _____ .... ?

2 Have you still got that book

   a _____ .... ?

   b _____ .... ?

   c _____ .... ?

3 Wasn't it Elizabeth

   a _____ .... ?

   b _____ .... ?

   c _____ .... ?

4 Which is the month

   a _____ .... ?

   b _____ .... ?

   c _____ .... ?

> you wanted to have off ~~~~ author I can never remember the name of
> lived in China until she was 16
> had to be invented to make the year longer
> mayor was arrested for corruption ~~~~ was reviewed in the *Times* last week
> the restaurant sacked for being rude to customers
> ~~was featured in that TV documentary last week~~
> most people get married ~~~~ I lent you last term
> was almost completely destroyed during the war
> Richard Burton was born ~~~~ boyfriend wants to go and live in Italy

STUDY TIP ▶ Relative pronouns

- *who/which* can be used with both defining and non-defining relative clauses
- *that* is not used in non-defining relative clauses
- *whom* is very rare nowadays, particularly in spoken English
- it is very common to omit the relative pronoun wherever possible

2.1 Future time clauses

Complete the following passage by putting the time conjunctions from the bubble in the correct space. The first one is shown as an example.

> until ~~~~ when
> by the time
> ~~before~~ ~~~~ if ~~~~ after
> while ~~~~ as soon as
> until ~~~~ once

Memorandum from Security Supervisor I B Shadow

1 ......*Before*........ the Ambassador arrives, you will have searched the embassy and grounds for anything suspicious. 2 .... he steps out of his bullet-proof limousine, you and three of your men will be in charge of his personal safety 3 .... he gets back into his limousine after the meeting. 4 .... he's shaken hands with the British diplomats, one of you will have to stay very close to him 5 .... he greets the well-wishers in the crowd and, remember, 6 .... you see anyone behaving strangely, you'll be expected to act first and ask questions later. 7 .... he goes inside the embassy building with the negotiators, you'll accompany him to the meeting room door and wait outside 8 .... he re-emerges – this could take anything from two to three hours.

9 .... he comes out of the embassy, the crowd will probably have dwindled somewhat but this is the time when you and your men will need to be most vigilant, so keep him covered all the time. 10 .... he gets back in his limousine, he'll be back In the hands of the mobile security unit and you'll be able to breathe a sigh of relief.

2.2 Guess the ending

Complete these sentences in a logical way. Look at the example provided.

1 Don't worry, you'll recognise me as soon as *you see me!*

2 It's OK, I'll wait for you until ....

3 I'll go and have a cup of tea while ....

4 Hurry up, or they'll have finished dinner by the time .... !

5 I'll meet you back here after we ....

6 Won't you get a fine if .... ?

7 Come on, let's do the washing-up before we ....

8 You won't feel much on this side of your mouth until the injection ....

3 Present tenses

Put the verbs in brackets into either the present simple or the present continuous tense. Put any other words in the brackets in the correct place. The first one has been done for you.

1 This milk *doesn't smell* (not smell) too fresh – I think I'll throw it out.

2 You .... (forever/use) my razor, can't you buy one of your own?

3 Oh yes, Jean and I .... (know) each other very well.

4 Mark .... (go) to work by train while his car's at the mechanic's.

5 Don't forget the coach .... (leave) at 6.45 tomorrow morning so you'd better get an early night.

6 Where's Harry? In the study, I think he .... (write) some letters.

7 Aunt Agnes is very generous, she .... (always/give) the children wonderful presents for their birthdays.

8 That new postman .... (not seem) very bright to me, he .... (always/leave) our letters in the wrong letterbox.

9 I'm sorry we can't make it to the party on Saturday but we .... (have) dinner with some old friends.

10 Predictably, at the end of the film the Swarzenegger hero .... (rescue) the prisoners and .... (get) the girl!

11 Where .... you .... (live) until your new house is ready?

12 Carter .... (serve), Pampas .... (return) but the ball .... (go) into the net. Game to Carter!

4 No matter …

Match the first part of each sentence in column **A** with the second part in column **B** and add a suitable word to complete it. Look at the example.

A

1 No matter .....how.....hard I try, ☐F☐
2 Well, it looks as though we'll have to buy a new one, ☐
3 She never gets to work on time, ☐
4 Don't trust her an inch, ☐
5 No matter .... much he'd like to, ☐
6 No matter .... you get there, ☐
7 No matter .... the doctor tells him, ☐
8 Cigarettes are extremely bad for you, ☐
9 Look, this rumour is totally untrue, ☐
10 Come on, you'd better clear up this mess, ☐

B

A no matter .... she promises.
B no matter .... it costs.
C he'll never forget the crash.
D no matter .... fault it was.
E he refuses to give up eating fatty food.
F I never lose any weight.
G no matter .... told you.
H no matter .... bus she takes.
I give us a ring to let us know everything's OK.
J no matter .... little tar they might contain.

5 Grammatical terms

Choose the correct grammatical term from the bubble below for each of the underlined words in the letter on page **14**. You will have to use some of the terms more than once. Look at the example provided.

> preposition   article   adjective
> pronoun   conjunction   noun
> base form   auxiliary verb   participle
> -ing noun   adverb   modal

Pick Strawberry Fields for the heritage beat

From Mr Gerald Murphy

1 Sir: <u>While</u> respecting Mark Haines' undoubted love of Britain's ancient 'Heritage' (Letters, 21 June), I would 2 like to assure <u>him</u> that there is much to admire in Britain's post-war cultural contribution to the modern world. 3 Just <u>ask</u> some of the thousands of tourists who come to Liverpool, to 4 visit the ancestral and <u>stately</u> homes of the four Beatles. 5 My experience as <u>a</u> Beatleguide in 6 the city <u>has</u> taught me that there is room for all points of view, and that foreign tourists welcome any chance to observe modern historic sites like 'Strawberry Fields' and the 'Eleanor 7 Rigby' headstone <u>in</u> St Peter's churchyard, Woolton, while pondering on the sandstone magnificence of the church architecture, and <u>reflecting</u> on 8 the meeting of Lennon and McCartney in July 1957 at that self-same site.

Tourism is changing, <u>for</u> a new 9 generation <u>now</u> walks the highways of 10 England. <u>They</u> are not snobs, they are 11 here to view the <u>making</u> of the British 12 nation in all its senses. More often than not, they listen to the musical <u>soundtrack</u> of British musicians, of 13 whom we <u>should</u> be proud, for it is, in 14 many cases, those musicians who brought these people to England in <u>the</u> first place. 15
<u>Sincerely</u>, 16
GERALD MURPHY
Project Co-ordinator
Northern Song Project
Birkenhead, Merseyside

1 While = *conjunction*

2 him = ...

3 ask = ...

4 stately = ...

5 a = ...

6 has = ...

7 in = ...

8 reflecting = ...

9 for = ...

10 now = ...

11 They = ...

12 making = ...

13 soundtrack = ...

14 should = ...

15 the = ...

16 Sincerely = ...

6 Wordcheck – Pastimes

Fill in the missing words in the grid below to reveal another word closely associated with them. Look at the example given.

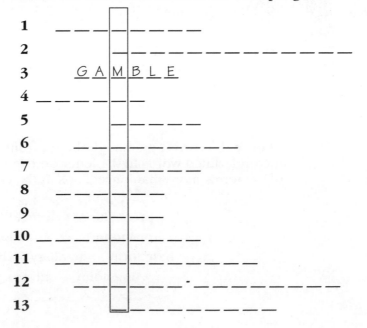

1 Talking in an informal way.

2 You must avoid these if you want to make the most of your time.

3 What you do with your money on a fruit machine or in a casino.

4 Small, ingenious machine or device people often play with, for example a pocket computer.

5 Board game with black and white pieces, including kings and queens.

6 Word puzzle in which you write your answers in little white boxcs.

7 Flat, round pieces you use in some board games, also the name for serving places in a shop.

8 A picture cut into irregular shapes that you put back together again.

9 You must know the answer to these to complete number 6.

10 What the dedicated, modern gardener uses to keep his/her grass short.

11 A difficult, intriguing problem or puzzle.

12 Looking at things on display in the shops without buying them.

13 Talking, often critically, about other people and their private affairs.

Unit 3

1 Gerunds

In each of the following sentences add a suitable subject made from a verb. The first one is shown as an example.

1 *Drinking lots of water* is supposed to be good for your complexion.

2 .... causes a lot of unnecessary accidents every year.

3 .... is much less popular now than it was twenty years ago.

4 .... is by far the most common way of spending the evening.

5 .... often makes you appreciate the things you took for granted in your own country.

6 .... crossword puzzles is a classic time-eater.

7 .... is a good way of losing weight and getting fit.

8 .... in poor light can damage your eyesight.

9 .... is my favourite way of relaxing.

10 .... is a sign of nervousness or stress.

2 Preposition + ...ing

Complete the following sentences by adding the correct preposition and a suitable gerund. Look at the example provided.

1 I'm really looking forward *to meeting* your sister, I've heard so much about her.

2 We're thinking .... to Turkey this summer.

3 Arnold was falsely accused .... cash from the till.

4 When I was a child my mother was always warning me .... lifts from strangers.

5 Jean doesn't believe .... today what she can put off until tomorrow!

6 Trevor is absolutely hopeless .... photos – he always cuts your head or feet off!

7 Lesley's rather anxious .... the doctor next week – she thinks it might be something serious.

8 Emma was furious with me .... her ex-boyfriend to the party.

9 Anyone interested .... on the trip to Bath should tell Kerry by noon today.

10 I'm tired .... the same old faces every day – I need a change!

11 I intend to find out who's responsible .... the window.

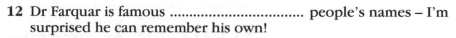

12 Dr Farquar is famous .... people's names – I'm surprised he can remember his own!

13 Carol is incredibly honest. She'd never dream .... a lie.

14 You can delete anything you don't want .... this button.

15 Sally found it difficult to re-adjust to the British way of life .... back from a long holiday in the Greek islands.

16 What's the name of that stuff you use .... grass stains out of clothes?

17 MANUFACTURER'S WARNING: Always wear safety goggles .... this machinery.

18 You must check in your mirror .... another car on the motorway.

3 ...ing or infinitive

Complete the following sentences with either a gerund or infinitive. In some cases the verb to use is indicated in the brackets. The first one has been done for you.

1 You'll remember to fill the car up with petrol, won't you?

2 Try .... a cup of camomile tea before you go to bed.

3 She remembered .... his face in a police identikit picture.

4 You must try .... down on the number of cigarettes you smoke.

5 Being a doctor means .... very long hours and .... a fragmented social life.

6 During the meeting we came .... that not only were we not getting a pay rise but probably a pay cut!

7 I regret .... him he was pathetic, I got a bit angry, that's all.

8 I regret .... you that there is very little chance of recovery.

9 Having defeated the champion in the opening match, she went on .... the tournament.

10 Isn't it time you stopped .... on your parents so much and tried .... on your own two feet?

11 You can't expect .... the exam if you spend all day .... video games.

12 I can't help .... (wonder) why Julie keeps .... home so late.

13 Would you mind not .... in here? I can't stand .... in other people's cigarette smoke.

14 Don't forget .... the car to the garage on Monday – the brakes need .... again.

15 There was no point in .... (promise) .... (help) if you don't like .... your hands dirty!

STUDY TIP ▶ **-ing form**

- Remember the rule that a preposition is always followed by an *-ing* form. All phrasal verbs must be followed by *-ing*:

e.g. I prefer reading to watching TV.
We're looking forward to seeing you.

- Keep a special note of verbs/expressions which take *-ing* after the preposition *to*:

e.g. I'm used to getting up early in the morning.

4 ...ing nouns

Put the nouns in the bubble below in the correct places in the following sentences. Some nouns need to be changed to the plural form. Look at the example given.

> showing   sighting
> saying   setting   awakening
> spelling   carving   hanging
> following   fitting   airing
> being   hearing
> recording   reading

1 Last century people used to attend public hangings outside local jails.

2 We'll need to leave work early if we want to see the earlier .... of 'Jurassic Park'.

3 The rock group 'U2' has a very large .... all over the world.

4 Have there ever been any verified .... of the Loch Ness monster?

5 I like to throw open the windows and give the room a good .... every morning.

6 Our second .... this evening comes from the poetic works of Oscar Wilde.

7 There's a lot of truth in the .... 'Everything comes to him who waits'.

8 We bought a beautiful wooden .... of a horse in Hungary.

9 The cabins were in the most attractive .... , on the edge of a lake, surrounded by forest.

10 He felt a gradual .... of love for this strange, independent girl.

11 There was an official .... to discover who was responsible for polluting the river.

12 I'm sorry it's so crackly but it's the original 1948 concert ....

13 He told me he'd spoken to some alien ....from another universe!

14 The bathroom still has all the original Victorian ....

15 Actually, the word has two different .... and both are correct!

5 ... ing adjectives

Match each adjective in column **A** with the appropriate noun in column **B**. The first one is shown as an example.

A		**B**
1 carving	G	**A** board
2 shaving	☐	**B** rod
3 building	☐	**C** bag
4 diving	☐	**D** stone
5 watering	☐	**E** licence
6 parking	☐	**F** powder
7 driving	☐	**G** knife
8 filling	☐	**H** can
9 paving	☐	**I** water
10 walking	☐	**J** site
11 fishing	☐	**K** cream
12 sleeping	☐	**L** space
13 ironing	☐	**M** station
14 washing	☐	**N** stick
15 drinking	☐	**O** board

STUDY TIP ▶ Collocations/word partnerships

- Some words in English are very useful in forming word partnerships e.g. *board*, *card*, *bag*.

diving	credit	carrier
chopping BOARD	membership CARD	shoulder BAG
chess	birthday	shopping

- Keep a record of these and other such useful words and their possible partners.

6 Cause and effect

Match the beginning of each sentence in column **A** with the correct ending in column **B** and add any necessary words. Look at the example.

A

1 Careless driving ☐
2 Eating too many sugary things ☐
3 Skin cancer ☐
4 Heart attacks ☐
5 One .... of using a computer all day ☐
6 Bad posture ☐
7 A sudden rise in temperature ☐
8 Malaria can .... from ☐
9 Obesity can be the .... of ☐
10 Crimes in inner cities have increased ☐
11 Letting children always do what they want ☐
12 Accidents in the home ☐

B

A overeating and lack of exercise.
B can be .... to tiredness and distraction.
C can and does .... in tooth decay.
D is to cause headaches and eye problems.
E being bitten by a mosquito.
F is a major .... of chronic back pain.
G .... of high unemployment and a lack of recreational facilities.
H can be .... by sunbathing for long periods.
I is a major ......*cause*...... of road accidents.
J can and does .... to behavioural problems at school.
K have increased as a .... of our modern stressful lifestyles.
L can and does .... avalanches.

7.1 Wordcheck – Stress and relaxation

Underline the word in each group that does not fit in with the other three. Use a dictionary to help you if necessary. The first one is shown as an example.

1	fun	enjoyable	<u>friendly</u>	light-hearted
2	nap	rush	snooze	siesta
3	wriggle	grip	grasp	clench
4	headache	sore neck	ulcer	symptom
5	protect	unwind	resist	defend
6	toes	arteries	thighs	calves
7	tense	angry	upset	vulnerable
8	exhale	sigh	stroke	breathe

7.2 Word partners

Match up the word partners in columns **A** and **B** as in the example.

A		**B**
1 blood	C	**A** night
2 hardening	☐	**B** mechanism
3 stress	☐	**C** pressure
4 balanced	☐	**D** point
5 sleepless	☐	**E** arteries
6 pressure	☐	**F** treatment
7 effective	☐	**G** diet
8 defence	☐	**H** management

Unit 4

1 Conditionals 1 and 2

Complete the following conditional sentences with suitable phrases. Look at the example given.

1 OK, OK, I'll lend you the money as long as you *pay me back* next week.

2 What would you do if your car .... miles from anywhere?

3 Quite frankly, I think you're going to fail the exam unless .... harder.

4 I know he's hardly ever around these days but if you .... tell him to get back in touch.

5 But supposing our train is late, how .... the airport on time?

6 I can't get to sleep at night unless .... a hot drink.

7 If my boyfriend spoke to me like that, ... his face.

8 You can borrow my video camera on condition that .... properly.

9 I'd apply for that job as an interpreter if .... better Russian.

10 Should .... further information, please contact our publicity officer.

11 I'm sure you .... those headaches all the time if you wore your glasses more often.

12 Suppose .... on a desert island, how would you survive?

13 I'd go and see the doctor with that rash if .... you.

14 We should be able to play tennis on Friday afternoon unless ...., of course.

15 I'd play a lot more sport if I .... so much work to do.

STUDY TIP ▶ **Conditionals**

- Although you can't use *'ll* after *if* in most conditional sentences, there is one time when you can. This is to express willingness or volition:

e.g. If you'll clear the table, I'll wash the plates.

22

2 Order of adjectives

Some of the adjectives in the following sentences are in the wrong order. Make any necessary corrections as in number one.

1 We were shown round the museum by a little, old, (friendly) woman who didn't speak much English.

2 Rob and Sally have bought a delightful old-fashioned country cottage just outside Cheltenham.

3 Where did you buy that round strange Persian rug you've got in the hall?

4 My sister wore an extraordinary large straw orange hat to the party.

5 Have you seen those tiny new amazing wrist TV's that you wear like a watch?

6 There was a beautiful antique French writing desk at the sale but it was too expensive for us.

7 Whatever happened to that red big American sports car you used to drive?

8 Have you read about that ingenious new surgical instrument for carrying out operations through a small opening in the skin?

9 The original Fiat 500, an incredibly little popular Italian car, is no longer in production.

10 The puppy had such round big lovely brown eyes that I couldn't help bringing him home with me.

STUDY TIP ▶ **Adjective order**

- A good way to remember adjective order is to memorise the phrase:

<u>V</u>ERY <u>S</u>OON <u>A</u> <u>T</u>RAIN <u>SH</u>OULD <u>C</u>OME

VALUE	SIZE	AGE	TEMPERATURE	SHAPE	COLOUR	ORIGIN	MATERIAL	+ NOUN
lovely	big	old	warm	round	red	Indian	cotton	cushion

---

3 Tenses

Decide which tense is being described in each 'time line' and short description and then write an example sentence in that tense. A cross shows an individual action or event and a wavy line shows an activity happening continuously or repeatedly. Look at the example given.

1 Past   Now   Future

←——— ×××××|××××× ———→ Tense = *Present Simple* ....

never changing/always true

e.g. I always brush my teeth before I go to bed.

2 Past   Now   Future

←——— ⌒⌒⌒⌒ ———→ Tense = ...

happening now/during a period around now

e.g. I .... this month.

3 Past   Now   Future

Tense = ...

past event where time is not mentioned or where the present result is more important than when the event happened

e.g. I .... so I'm not hungry, thanks.

4 Past   Now   Future

Tense = ...

*action started in past and **a)** continuing now **b)** finished but evidence remains*

e.g. **a)** I .... for an hour.
    b) I .... that's why my face is so red.

5 Past a)   b) Now   Future
    this time the phone
    last week rang

Tense = ...

*activity over time in past **a)** at a certain time **b)** when another event occurred*

e.g. **a)** I .... this time last week.
    b) I .... when the phone rang.

6 Past   Now   Future

Tense = ...

event(s) in past occurring before a point of reference/another event in past

e.g. By the time the police arrived, the robbers ....

7 Past   Now   Future

Tense = ...

activity started before and continuing up to a point of reference in past

e.g. I .... for ten hours when I fell asleep exhausted.

8 Past   Now   Future

Tense = ...

activity seen as occurring around a stated time/reference point in the future

e.g. I .... this time next month.

9 Past   Now   Future

Tense = ...

future event(s) happening before another future event/point of reference

e.g. I hope I .... when I meet her next week.

10 Past   Now   Future

Tense = ...

activity started before and continuing up to a future point of reference

e.g. I .... for three years next June.

4 Dictionary abbreviations

Give two examples for each of the following dictionary abbreviations. The first one has been done for you.

1 PREP with, from

2 ADV...

3 SUPERL ....

4 CONJ ....

5 PRON POSS ....

6 N[U] OR UNCOUNT ....

7 COMPAR ....

8 ADJ ....

9 NEG ....

10 PASS ....

> ## STUDY TIP ➤ Using a dictionary
>
> • As an advanced learner, you will find a good monolingual dictionary an essential tool. Apart from spelling and meanings, a dictionary can tell you:
> - pronunciation – if you can recognise phonetic script
> - word stress – (rɪˈtɜːn) or (rɪt ɜːn)
> - word formation
> - collocations
> - useful phrases the word is used in

---

5 Under and over

Fill in the spaces below with words beginning with *under* and their opposites. Look at the example provided.

Under ...

	WORD	OPPOSITE
1 of less than normal size (adj)	undersized	oversized
2 fail to recognise how clever, important or significant someone or something is (v)		
3 not expressing an idea fully or adequately (n)		
4 weak and unhealthy due to a lack of food (adj)		————
5 charge too little money for something (v)		
6 having too few people for the amount of work (adj)		

6 Report writing

You are writing a report for 'Bocia', the manufacturers of the new 'Bambo' pushchair, based on the results of interviews with mothers and fathers all over the country. The aim of the interviews was to find out how good the pushchair is. Expand the following notes into a full report using the phrases in the bubble below. You may also use subheadings e.g. Introduction, Observations, Recommendations, etc. Write about 250 words.

> The aim of this report is to … It was based on …
>
> It was found that … A/the majority/minority of people …
>
> In the words of … On the whole … It is interesting that …
>
> It is recommended that … It is advisable for 'Bocia' to …
>
> 'Bocia' might consider … To sum up/summarise … On balance …

Notes for report on new 'Bambo' pushchair

Number of people interviewed: 150
Interview locations: London, Bristol, Birmingham, Gloucester, Glasgow, Leeds.

Sample comments:

'Compared to our old pushchair, this is fantastic – it's so light and manageable.' Mrs Roberta Long, Gloucester

'My little boy really likes going out in it – so it must be comfy, mustn't it?' Mr Adam Blair, London

'Well, we quite like it but it's a bit stiff to open and close really. That's our only complaint.' Mr and Mrs Osmont, Leeds

'It folds up really small and fits in the boot of the car no problem. The only thing is it's always getting stuck in little holes.' Mrs Joy McCarthy, Glasgow

Analysis:

Good points	Bad points
– light	– difficult to open and close
– easy to steer	– wheels too small so it gets stuck in holes on rough ground
– good for carrying shopping	
– attractive design and colours	– wheels difficult to lock as mechanism is too small to operate by foot
– comfortable for baby	
– small when folded	
– 4 positions for baby, from sitting up to lying flat	

Suggestions (with diagram):

make opening hinge easier to open/close

increase size of wheels →

make wheel locking mechanism larger

7 Wordcheck – Teaching and learning

Complete this crossword. Look at the example given.

Across

1 A skill or particular way of doing something.

2 Aim, goal, objective.

3 and 5 If you have this, you can recall a perfect mental picture of what you have been learning.

4 It's important to do this before your exam.

6 A useful piece of advice to help you do something better.

7 A type of dictionary with two languages.

8 A job you have to do or complete.

9 If you don't know the answer, you can always .... !

10 The regular recurrence of stress in spoken English.

Down

11 Reinforce, make more solid or stronger.

12 Repeating things others say without understanding.

13 You take in or .... knowledge like a sponge takes in water.

14 Ways of studying to help you learn more effectively or quickly.

15 Abilities or talents you have which you haven't put into full use yet.

Progress Test One

Units 1 – 4

Check your progress by entering your score in the box at the end of each activity and at the end of the complete test.

1 Complete the following newspaper article by writing **one** word in each of the numbered gaps.

Shining example or white elephant?

The new university hospital in Trenton, **(1)** ....the Health Minister Victoria Culley has described **(2)** ....a 'shining example' to hospitals all **(3)**...................the country, has been open now for over six months. **(4)** .... heard several less than complimentary comments about the organisation and efficiency of the place, I decided to see for myself. Before **(5)**...................there, I had arranged with my local GP to have some routine blood tests for anaemia.

In **(6)** .... of arriving early (7.15 a.m.!), I found that there were already long queues at the reception desks. **(7)** .... I was waiting, I looked around and have to admit it is an impressive building; large and light with marble everywhere. Eventually my turn came and I presented my doctor's letter to the receptionist, **(8)** .... informed me I was in the x-ray queue and I'd have to go to another queue and start again! I couldn't believe it and asked her if it **(9)** .... be possible to give me an appointment card anyway **(10)** .... making me queue up again. She informed me it was no **(11)** .... arguing with her and I should have read the sign, an almost invisible piece of card saying 'X-Rays' just in front of her **(12)** ....very few people can have seen it. No **(13)** .... how hard I tried to persuade her, she wouldn't give me an appointment card for a blood test, so I started **(14)** .... again and finally got the card at 8.30! I then set off for the blood tests room, following the nice new signs **(15)**................... they suddenly stopped and I realised I was in a part of the hospital that hasn't been finished yet! When I got to the door I saw a notice saying 'Back in 10 minutes'. I sat down and waited for 30 minutes before a doctor appeared and told me to come in without, of course, **(16)** .... for keeping me waiting. I asked him why I'd had to wait and he explained he'd had to help out in another ward which was **(17)** .... as a **(18)**................... of a flu epidemic among the doctors!

I got out of the hospital at 9.45 a.m. and breathed a sigh of relief. I'm now waiting for the results.

So, Mrs Culley, a far from rosy picture. Certainly the public should be **(19)** .... no illusions that things have changed for the better. Perhaps you should visit the hospital as an anonymous out-patient rather than a government minister if you really want to know what it's like **(20)**..................., as I suspect, you don't actually care that much!

20

28

2 Fill in each blank with a suitable form of the word in brackets. Look at the example provided.

Example: Please be *careful* (care) or you'll break it.

1 A certain degree of stress seems to be .... (avoid) in modern life.

2 The steak was really .... (do) so I sent it back with instructions to cook it for another five minutes!

3 Many people say a lunch-time sleep .... (able) them to work better.

4 .... (anxious) prevents people learning effectively.

5 It's important to .... (solid) new information by going over it in your mind.

6 In Switzerland it's your legal .... (respond) to keep the pavement outside your house clear of snow.

7 Financial .... (secure) is a great source of stress for many people.

8 This is a very old game and there are .... (count) variations of it.

9 The new pocket calculator and diary really is an .... (value) aid to the memory.

10 Looking after young children can be extremely .... (stress)

10

3 Complete each of the following sentences with the appropriate form of a suitable phrasal verb. An example is provided.

Example: Dennis has given up his job so he can stay at home and *look after* the children.

1 Overeating and lack of exercise can .... serious health problems in later life.

2 Hi Brenda, Peter here. I'm just .... to say I've got two tickets for the concert on Saturday night. Fancy coming?

3 You should .... the pros and cons carefully before buying a second-hand car.

4 Now, don't .... us .... We're counting on you to cook something really special for the party this Saturday.

5 The group .... their concert with their greatest hit. So everyone went home happy!

5

4 Use the following notes to write about a pop group. You must use all the words in the same order as the notes. You may add words and change the form of the words where necessary but do not add any extra information. Look carefully at the example provided.

1 pop group – Surface Tension – famous – last year.

2 4 lads from Hereford – met university – studying Physics.

3 first hit – 'Closed Circuit' – Top 10 five weeks.

4 present – arranging tour Eastern Europe – start next month.

5 also – new album – 'Like Poles Repel' – release next month.

6 ambition – make it in USA – no hits so far.

7 lead singer – Rick Springer – says no girlfriend – no time!

8 others say – fairly settled – steady girlfriends.

9 back from Europe next year – 15 concerts UK.

The new British rock sensation!!!

1 The pop group 'Surface Tension' became famous last year.

2 ....

3 ....

4 ....

5 ....

6 ....

7 ....

8 ....

9 ....

15

TOTAL

50

Unit 5

1 Past simple vs. past continuous

In the following sentences put the verbs in brackets in either the past simple or past continuous tense. Put any other words in brackets in the correct place. Look at the example provided.

1 While the teacher was explaining (explain) the sum on the blackboard, the children were throwing (throw) paper aeroplanes around the classroom.

2 Eve ....(live) in Athens when she .... (meet) the man who was to become her husband.

3 .... you .... (not work) at McIlroy's when they .... (have) that terrible fire?

4 As it .... (get) foggier it .... (become) almost impossible to steer the boat along the narrow canal.

5 I .... (hear) a strange noise just as I .... (go) to sleep.

6 When the fire alarm .... (go) off, we .... (leave) the building as quickly as possible.

7 At the place where we .... (live) before, our neighbours .... (always/have) violent arguments late at night.

8 I .... (hope) you'd come round for tea one afternoon next week.

9 Fiona .... (live) in New York when her first novel .... (publish).

10 On looking out of the window, Dick .... (see) it was another dreary day. The wind .... (blow) hard and big black clouds .... (gather) on the horizon.

11 While the others .... (lie) on the beach, poor old Gary .... (work) in the office as usual.

12 When the phone .... (ring), she .... (pick) it up and .... (put) it down again!

13 I .... (never/understand) why you .... (always/get) to school late on Monday mornings.

14 Beverley .... (work) in a fast-food restaurant for a few months before she .... (go) to college.

15 When I .... (be) a lad, we .... (always/go) to Heysham for our summer holidays. I .... (really/love) the place even though it .... (often/rain)!

2.1 Phrasal verbs with 'up'

Substitute the underlined words in the sentences on page **32** with a phrasal verb with *up*. The first one is shown as an example.

1 The TV's rather quiet, can't you <u>increase its volume</u>/turn it up?

2 I'd like to <u>improve</u>/ .... my Spanish before going on holiday to Valencia.

3 There's not much point in wearing your anorak if you don't <u>close its zip</u>/ ....

4 What's the matter, Rupert? Can't you <u>fasten</u>/ .... your seatbelt for yourself?

5 The party started off rather formally but <u>got more lively</u>/............................ after an hour or so.

6 The police eventually managed to <u>bring together</u>/............................ all the criminals who had taken part in the bank robbery.

7 It looks a bit cloudy at the moment but I think it'll <u>become brighter</u>/ .... this afternoon.

8 Children often don't realise how cruel it is to <u>unite</u>/ .... against someone who is different from them.

9 The dog was so dangerous it had to be kept <u>attached to a chain</u>/ .... in the back yard.

10 Can't we <u>go a little faster</u>/ .... a bit or we'll never get there on time?

2.2 Can you split it up?

In the following sentences add a particle to complete the phrasal verb and an appropriate object pronoun (*it*, *me*, *them*, etc.) in the **correct** place – either before or after the particle. Look at the example provided.

1 OK, you read out the phone numbers and I'll jot *them down.*

2 That cheese in the fridge had gone off so I threw............... ....

3 He doesn't look like his father much but he takes .... in the way he behaves.

4 Their company has gone bankrupt and they only set .... two years ago!

5 Look, don't keep complaining to me about it. If your steak is underdone, send .... !

6 Did you believe that story about a long-lost brother? No, not a word of it. I'm sure she was making ....

7 What did little Patrick think of his first visit to the swimming pool? Oh, he took .... like a duck to water!

8 You don't have to give me an answer right now. Think............... .... for a few days before you decide.

9 The form was so complicated that she had to ask her accountant to fill .... for her.

10 I still don't understand this word and I've just looked .... in the dictionary!

11 As they didn't have anywhere to stay, we put .... for the night.

12 Nina fainted in the heat and we had to bring .... with smelling salts.

STUDY TIP ▶ Separable vs. inseparable phrasal verbs

- You **must** separate some phrasal verbs by putting the object pronoun (*me, her, us,* etc.) **between** the verb and particle not **after** the particle:

e.g. Suzie rang **me** up for a chat last night.

- Often, however, it is possible to put a full object (*the doctor, Percy,* etc.) either **between** the verb and particle or **after** the particle:

e.g. Suzie rang **the doctor** up to change her appointment.
    Suzie rang up **the doctor** to change her appointment.

- With other phrasal verbs, the object pronoun or full object goes **after** the particle.

e.g. Do you mind looking after **the children?**
    No, I love looking after **them.**

- If you are not sure if a phrasal verb must be separated or not, check in a dictionary.

2.3   In other words …

In the following story replace the words in brackets with an appropriate phrasal verb taken from the box below. Look at the example.

pull up	start up	go through with	look on to	pull off
build up	stub out	pull over	~~look out for~~	jump out of
	pull out	drop off	shoot off	take aback

THE HOLD-UP

The hold-up had started going wrong. Clyde, who was supposed to be **(1)** looking out for (waiting to see) the security van from a flat which **(2)** .... (had a view of) the main street, had **(3)** .... (gone) to sleep due to the fact that he had been drinking brandy all morning to **(4)** .... (increase) his courage.

So Bugsy, Danny and Studs were completely **(5)** .... (amazed) when the security van **(6)** .... (stopped) outside the bank without a word of warning from Clyde. Bugsy **(7)** ....(extinguished) his cigarette. 'We've got to **(8)** .... it (not leave unfinished) now – it's too late to **(9)**................................. (abandon a difficult plan)!'

Studs **(10)** .... (put in motion) the getaway car and **(11)** .... (moved) to a spot just past the bank. Bugsy and Danny **(12)** .... (quickly left) the car and **(13)** .... (ran) towards the bank.

Studs suddenly realised just how shaky he felt after the recent events and got out of the car for a breath of fresh air.

A few minutes later Bugsy and Danny came running back from the bank shouting to the still dazed Studs that they had **(14)** .... it .... (succeeded in a difficult plan). Studs, however, didn't seem too interested and stood glued to the spot where he had left the car.

'Good grief! Is nothing sacred these days? Some crook's just stolen the car.

> ## STUDY TIP ▶ Phrasal verbs
>
> - A good way to record and remember phrasal verbs is to group them according to particle (*up, down, in, out, on, off* etc.) rather than verb (*get, make, run* etc.):
>
> e.g.
>
> | turn | keep | |
> |------|------|---|
> | switch ON | put | UP WITH |
> | keep | catch | |
>
> - Remember that particles often have fixed meanings such as fastening and restriction, approach etc:
>
> e.g. wrap up, zip up, tie up, make for, head for

3 Expressing the future

Put the verbs in brackets in the most suitable form (active or passive) of the future. The first one has been done for you.

1 Are you *doing* (do) anything special on Friday evening?

2 Mandy .... (finish) her exams by this time next week.

3 The train .... (get) in at 5.15, which means we .... (have) about half an hour to get to the conference centre.

4 Look out! That boy ....(fall) off his bike!

5 The new sports centre ....(open) next month but I doubt if it .... (complete) by then!

6 The Prince .... (give) a speech to local community leaders this evening.

7 We .... (live) in this house for exactly five years next Sunday.

8 Congratulations! We hope you .... (be) very happy together.

9 The play ....(not start) until 8.30 so I think we .... (have) time to eat something first.

10 Anna looks rather fat these days. Oh, don't you know? She .... (have) a baby.

11 Just think, this time on Thursday we ....(fly) to Los Angeles.

12 Don't worry, I........................ (phone) the plumber first thing tomorrow morning.

13 Do you think you .... (finish) that report by the end of the week?

14 .... I .... (give) you a lift to the airport on Monday or ....Fred........................ (take) you?

15 We'd better hurry up, I think they.. (close).

4.1 Wordcheck – Air travel

Use a dictionary to help you mark the stress patterns in the underlined words below. Draw one circle for each syllable and show the stressed syllable with a large circle. Be careful to identify the grammatical function in each case. Look at the example provided.

1 Oh no, I've left my handbag at the <u>check-in</u> desk.

2 The <u>steward</u> on the plane gave us some sweets to suck before <u>take-off.</u>

3 Would late passengers for flight BY577 please <u>check in</u> immediately.

4 <u>Lavatories</u> on planes are usually rather small.

5 The bus for the city centre leaves from outside the <u>terminal</u> building.

6 Please have your <u>boarding card</u> ready.

7 I'm not sure if I'll be leaving today as I've got a <u>standby</u> ticket.

8 Sorry for the <u>delay</u>, we hope to <u>take off</u> in five minutes.

STUDY TIP ▶ Word stress

- Use bubbles not accents to show the correct stress on words you have difficulty with. Bubbles show not only the main stress but also the number of syllables which are actually pronounced:

e.g. comfortable   interesting   temperature

4.2 Wordsearch

There are **15** words connected with air travel in the box below. You will find 7 horizontally, 4 vertically and 4 diagonally. Three have been found for you.

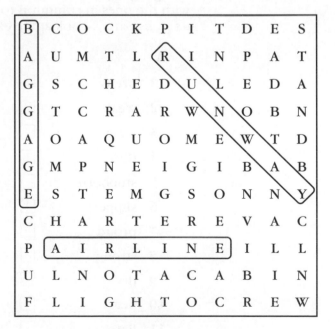

Unit 6

1.1 Comparisons

Complete the following sentences with a suitable comparative or superlative form of the words in brackets. Look at the example given.

1 According to a computer, Spanish is (easy) *the easiest* foreign language to learn.

2 Dogs are intelligent but not (intelligent) .... chimpanzees.

3 They say it's (good) .... to have loved and lost than never to have loved at all.

4 Even (carefully) ....prepared plans can go wrong.

5 England isn't (mountainous country) .... Scotland.

6 Reykjavik is the world's (northern) .... capital city.

7 Your composition is full of mistakes because you didn't spend half (time) .... on it .... you should have!

8 Don't worry, you'll be OK with Gerry, he's (careful driver) .... you could wish to have.

9 In the Alto Adige region of Italy, German dialect is spoken much (frequently) .... Italian.

10 Sumo wrestlers must be (heavy) .... athletes in the world.

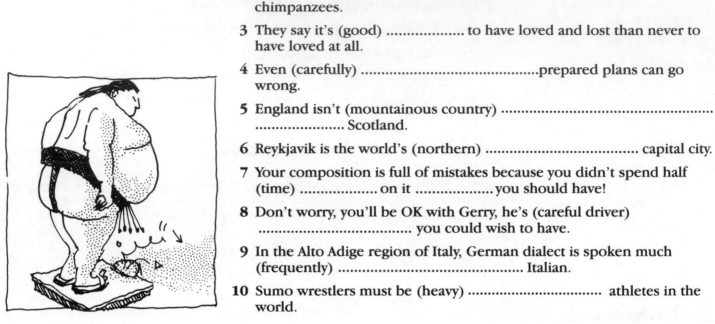

1.2 As good as gold

Using a good monolingual dictionary, check which words in column **A** go with the ones in column **B** to form common comparative expressions with *as ... as (a)* .... Look at the example provided.

A		**B**
1 pretty	G	A a pancake
2 weak	☐	B a bat
3 fresh	☐	C a kitten
4 thin	☐	D a bone
5 stubborn	☐	E an eel
6 slippery	☐	F a daisy
7 proud	☐	G a picture
8 strong	☐	H a mule
9 dry	☐	I an ox
10 deaf	☐	J a rake
11 flat	☐	K a peacock
12 blind	☐	L a post

36

1.3   Complete the sentences

Now complete the following sentences with the expressions you have made. The first one has been done for you.

1 Doesn't little Amy look nice in her new dress?
Oh yes, she's as pretty as a picture!

2 Alf is .... , he can't see much without his glasses.

3 Oh no! We'll have to change the tyre, it's ....

4 If we don't get some rain soon, we'll never grow anything in the garden, it's ....

5 I had a good night's sleep last night, so I'm .... this morning.

6 I wouldn't give Colin any of my money to invest, he's ....

7 Tim's been in bed all week with flu and he's ....

8 Freda's .... , once she makes up her mind she's going to do something, nothing you can say will stop her!

9 My word! David's lost a lot of weight.
Yes. Do you think he's OK? He looks .... to me!

10 Mrs Copley's daughter has been offered a place at university.
Yes and she's .... She's already told half the town.

11 Young Alan is really helpful on the farm. He's .... and he'll do anything you ask him to.

12 I'm afraid Grandad won't hear you unless you shout. He's ....!

2   Dramatic inversion

Complete the following sentences to make a more dramatic version of the sentence printed above it. The first one has been done for you.

1 You mustn't press this red button under any circumstances.
Under no circumstances *must you press this red button.*

2 She'd only just stubbed out one cigarette when she lit another.
Hardly ....

3 We didn't see a soul all day.
Not ....

4 As soon as I put the phone down, it rang again!
No sooner ....

5 He spoke so quietly that I didn't hear a thing he said.
So ....

6 They didn't win a game all season.
   Not ....

7 Life is like that.
   Such ....

8 She didn't realise who he was until she'd been speaking to him for ten minutes.
   Only after ....

9 Kate not only spilled wine on the carpet but she also broke six glasses.
   Not only ....

10 I'd never seen such a gigantic fish before!
   Never ....

3 Like, as and alike

Put *like*, *as* or *alike* in the appropriate places in the following sentences.
One is shown as an example.

1 Several of the businessmen got a little rowdy and started behaving like complete idiots.

2 Just .... I suspected, my letter had been delivered to the wrong office.

3 The Watkins brothers are really .... , aren't they?
   Yes, just .... two peas in a pod.

4 Nothing can go wrong providing you do exactly .... you're told.

5 The fundamental injustice of the law was that it did not treat all offenders ....

6 There's no need to talk .... that in front of the children!

7 .... they had feared, the company decided to make 200 workers redundant.

8 Cheryl must have been terrified. She came running out of the house .... a bat out of hell!

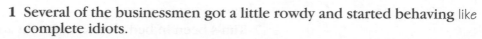

STUDY TIP	as vs. like

● Another useful distinction between these two is:

as = in the capacity of

e.g. She works as a taxi driver.
     He used his briefcase as a table to rest his notes on.

like = similar to

e.g. She works like a beaver.
     He's got a briefcase like yours.

4 Linking and logical devices – addition, concession, contrast

Complete the following sentences with suitable linking devices. An asterisk (*) indicates at least two possible answers. Look at the example.

1 Jenny speaks * both/not only Russian and/but also excellent Chinese.

2 .... does Jenny speak Russian, ... excellent Chinese.

3 Jenny speaks Russian. *..........................., she speaks excellent Chinese.

4 *........................... speaking Russian, Jenny speaks excellent Chinese.

5 They looked at us *........................... we came from another planet!

6 *........................... the doctor told him to rest for a week, he was back at work after two days.

7 .... we'd caught the earlier train we wouldn't have got there on time. So, stop worrying!

8 I know she's a sensible girl and .... I can't help worrying about her.

9 They played golf all morning *........................... the torrential rain.

10 We thought it was going to be a great match. ...., it turned out to be rather dull.

11 They've got no chance of winning the game; .... , they're training every day.

12 Some people like boxing, *........................... others absolutely detest it.

STUDY TIP ➤ **even if vs. even though**

- Remember that *even if* is used before statements that are hypothetical i.e. not fact:

e.g. Even **if** I had all the money in the world, I wouldn't buy that car.
We wouldn't have caught the plane even **if** we'd taken a taxi.

- *Even though*, on the other hand, is used before statements that are fact:

e.g. She's not happy with her job even **though** she's just had a pay rise and promotion.
He went to the cinema with his friends even **though** he'd already seen the film.

---

5 Informal letters

In the following letter, there are 7 mistakes of layout and style. One has been marked for you. There are also 7 missing phrases. Find the other 6 mistakes and complete the 7 missing phrases.

Andy Kulmbacher
▼ Bramley Road (25)
Burnville BV2 6BZ

23rd Oct, 19—

Dear friend,
it was very nice to (1) .... after such a long time.
(2) .... to hear that you've settled down in your new job in Valencia and are getting into the local way of life!

As you know, I'm still working at the same language school as before although I'm now in charge of marketing our courses in Europe! So it's a lot more responsibility and lots of travelling. As it happens, I'm coming to Valencia next month and (3) .... favour. I desperately need the names, addresses and phone numbers of the directors of all the local English language schools and I can't seem to get that sort of information in this country. (4) .... if you could go through the local yellow pages and send me the information. Please don't (5) .... if you can't manage it, I can always do it when I get there.

(6) .... , we must definitely meet up when I'm over. (7) .... see you soon.

Looking forward to hearing from you. Yours sincerely,
Andy

6 Wordcheck – Language

Complete the missing words in the following sentences. The first one has been done for you.

1 A lingua franca is a language adopted for local communication in an area where several different languages are spoken.

2 Comma, full stop and question mark are all examples of p ....

3 Your first language is also called your m........................ ....

4 The levels of formality and informality in a language are known as r........................ .

5 Jargon is a particular language used by a few people to talk about specialised subjects whereas s........................ refers to very informal everyday words and expressions used by many people.

6 In many countries English is the o .... of law and education even though the common people speak a different language.

7 It's often impossible to give the appropriate meaning of a word unless you know the c........................it's in.

8 The symbols used to write a language are called the s........................

Unit 7

1 Degrees of comparison

Using the language in the boxes below, complete the comparisons between the two couples as in the example.

slightly much/far considerably a great deal	more/less/fewer	nearly about exactly over	twice half 5 times	as much as as many as

MARTIN   FIONA   RUPERT   RACHEL

	MARTIN	FIONA	RUPERT	RACHEL
Age	39	42	37	29
Height	1m 77cm	1m 40cm	1m 76cm	1m 65cm
Weight	96kg	48kg	75kg	59kg
Working day	9 hrs	5.5 hrs	6 hrs	3 hrs
Annual income	£21,000	£8,250	£16,000	£4,000
Exercise per week	1hr	2 hrs	4 hrs	1.5 hrs

1 (AGE) Rachel is *considerably younger than* Fiona.

2 (AGE) Martin is .... Rupert.

3 (WEIGHT) Fiona weighs .... Martin.

4 (WEIGHT) Martin weighs .... Rupert.

5 (HEIGHT) Rupert is .... Martin.

6 (HEIGHT) Fiona is .... Rachel.

7 (WORK) Martin works .... Rachel.

8 (WORK) Fiona works .... Rupert.

9 (INCOME) Rachel earns .... Fiona.

10 (INCOME) Martin earns .... Rachel.

11 (EXERCISE) Rupert takes .... Martin.

12 (EXERCISE) Rachel takes .... Fiona.

41

2 Would rather

Complete the first sentence using some form of *would rather* for each of the following two-line dialogues. Look at the example provided.

1 A: I'd rather you didn't have your TV on so loud in the evenings.

   B: Oh, sorry. I'll turn the volume down after 10 p.m.

2 A: Would ....?

   B: Um, a pizza, I think. I'm fed up with curry.

3 A: Sally'd ....

   B: Would she? Sorry, I didn't think she'd mind. Oh well, I'll take him outside and leave him in the car. Come on, Rover!

4 A: Would ....?

   B: Well, yes, I would really. I mean she's not very good at keeping a secret, is she!

5 A: Would ....?

   B: Well, yes. Then I could have got your bed ready and bought some more food.

6 A: I'd ....

   B: Oh yeah, me too. It's really boring to watch but great fun when you're playing.

7 A: Would ....?

   B: Oh no, I'm quite tired and it's nice to stay in and watch television sometimes.

8 A: I'd ....

   B: Oh come on, don't be stupid he won't mind. It's his job to come and visit sick people, even at night!

3 Present perfect simple and continuous

In the following sentences decide whether to use the present perfect simple, the present perfect continuous or the past simple tense of the verbs in brackets and fill in any other missing words as in the example.

1 How long *have* you *been running* (run) the hotel *for* now?

2 When .... you .... (see) the doctor? I .... (not see) him yet.

3 I .... (know) Lily .... about a year. She's great fun!

4 Why .... Nick .... (study) so hard recently? .... he .... (fail) his last exams?

5 .... Rob .... (finish) his novel? Oh yes, it .... just .... (be) published.

6 They .... (live) in that same little house .... the day they .... (get) married 20 years ago. I don't think they'll move now!

7 What a fantastic old car! How long ....you ....(have) it?

8 Where's Janet? I ....(look) for her all morning – ....she..................(leave) the office?

9 I see they still ....(not repair) that big hole in the road.

10 The team .... (not win) a single match so far this season.

11 You're looking very fit and healthy these days! .... you ....(do) a lot of exercise?

12 .... Maisy ....(phone) yet? Yes, about ten minutes ago. She..................(say) she can't make it tonight.

13 How many of those chocolates ....you .... (eat) so far?

14 We ....(use) my father's garage as a storeroom for our furniture .... the fire. We still .... (not find) anywhere permanent to live.

15 Julie .... (eat) nothing but 'paella'..................her trip to Spain last month!

4 Dictionary skills

In all of the following exercises you should use a good English/English dictionary to help you find the answers.

A Parts of speech

Decide the grammatical function of each of the underlined words.

1 The <u>poor</u> are always with us.

2 Sorry, I'm afraid I explained that rather <u>poorly.</u>

3 Many students are quite <u>poor.</u>

4 Jack's feeling rather <u>poorly</u> so he's staying at home today.

B Connotation

In the following sentences, decide on the different meanings of the underlined words and if they are being used to give a positive, negative, or neutral connotation.

5 Phil has got incredibly <u>hairy</u> forearms, hasn't he.

6 It was rather <u>hairy</u> coming down the mountain road with no lights on the car.

7 Anna's really <u>funny</u>, she just makes me laugh and laugh!

8 I thought there was something a bit <u>funny</u> about his explanation of the accident.

9 In spite of the forecast, it turned out to be a <u>fine</u> day.

10 As a restorer of old paintings, she must have an eye for <u>fine</u> detail.

C Collocation (word partners)

Match the things in column **A** with the noises they make in column **B**.

A		B	
11	leaf	**A**	moans
12	floorboard	**B**	ticks
13	clock	**C**	howls
14	water	**D**	squeals
15	wind	**E**	rumbles
16	brake	**F**	wails
17	thunder	**G**	rustles
18	small bell	**H**	gushes
19	sick person	**I**	creaks
20	siren	**J**	tinkles

D Word formation (derivations)

Use the correct form of the word *use* in each sentence.

21 Haven't you got another dictionary? This one's absolutely ....!

22 The computer disks got wet so they were no longer ....

23 Before buying a .... car, it's a good idea to have it checked by a mechanic.

24 .... of the photocopier are kindly requested to report any breakdowns to the secretary.

25 I think your time could be more .... spent than reading comics all day!

STUDY TIP ▶ Word formation

● It is a good idea to record 'difficult' words in groups with the same ending:

e.g. friendship, hardship, leadership

   neighbourhood, childhood, boyhood

   witchcraft, handicraft

E Pronunciation and stress

For sentences **26** to **30** cross out the silent letters. For **31** to **35**, draw bubbles to show the correct stress e.g. córrèct.

26 buoy   **27** wrestling   **28** knock   **29** comb   **30** sword

31 guitar   **32** photographer   **33** difficulty   **34** calculator   **35** original

STUDY TIP ▶ Silent letters

- It is useful to know that silent letters often occur in fixed combinations:

e.g.
- co<u>mb</u> du<u>mb</u> thu<u>mb</u>
- <u>wr</u>ong <u>wr</u>ap <u>wr</u>angle
- li<u>st</u>en whi<u>st</u>le fa<u>st</u>en
- an<u>sw</u>er <u>sw</u>ord

- Keep a list of words that fall into such groups.
- When in doubt, check in your dictionary.

5 Wordcheck – Food and health

Complete this crossword. An example is given.

Across

4 Liquids obtained from plants (e.g. olives) used in cooking. (4)

7 How long you live. (8)

9 Eating no meat. (10)

10 Sea creatures, with hard skins or shells, which we eat e.g. crabs. (9)

13 Milk and products derived from it are known as .... products. (5)

14 Dangerous substance produced in the blood due to eating fatty food. (11)

15 Often used instead of butter – usually made from vegetable fats. (9)

Down

1 Long life. (9)

2 Green vegetable famous for keeping you fit and healthy – used by Popeye. (7)

3 Greasy substances found in meat products now considered very bad for your health. (6 and 4)

5 Edible fish from the sea. (7)

6 White grain used as food practically everywhere. (4)

8 You break open the hard shell and eat what's inside. (3)

11 The organ of the body most seriously affected by a bad diet. (5)

12 Cereals, brown bread, fruit and nuts contain a lot of this substance which helps food move more quickly through your body. (5).

Unit 8

1 Modal verbs

Complete the following sentences with a suitable form of *can, could, be able, may, might, must* and the verb in brackets. An example is given.

1 I feel absolutely awful. I think I must have (have) flu.

2 Are you going to .... (come) to Charlie's birthday party next Saturday?

3 My word! It .... (take) you ages to write all this. There are more than 2,000 pages!

4 Which bus do you think you .... (leave) your bag on?

5 It's odd we haven't received that cheque. Showerings said they'd sent it.

Yes, I suppose it .... (get) lost in the post but I doubt it.

6 I .... (swim) really well when I was six years old.

7 Although she had a broken leg, she .... (swim) to the shore.

8 You .... (tell) me it was a formal party. I looked a real idiot in my pullover and jeans!

9 It's not surprising we .... (not find) the house. You gave us the wrong address!

10 I used to .... (run) for miles. Now I .... (not even run) round the block!

11 I wonder why Pam ignored me in the street this morning.

Well, she .... (not realise) it was you. She's as blind as a bat.

12 Smoking .... (cause) all sorts of physical problems.

13 We .... (not be) more delighted when we heard the news. Congratulations!

14 Quick, Phil! .... you (see) that man over there? I think he .... well (be) the one the police are looking for.

15 Marsha .... (be) a brilliant lawyer but she gave it all up to go and live in Nepal.

16 What's that there in those trees?
It .... (not be) a dog, it's too big. Let's run for it!

17 Jane's not completely deaf but she .... (not hear) properly for a long time.

18 Billy, come away from that dog. It .... (bite) you.

47

> **STUDY TIP** ▶ **could vs. was able to**
>
> ● Remember *could* is used to show **general ability** in the past:
>
> e.g. She could drive when she was 13.
>
> ● *Was able to* shows ability on a **specific occasion** in the past:
>
> e.g. Despite having a flat tyre, she was able to drive home.

2 Phrasal verbs

In the following passage most (but not all) of the phrasal verbs have either the wrong verb or wrong particle. If a correction is required, write it in the space provided. Look at the example.

Although £10 seemed a lot for a guided walking tour, I'd   **1** .... *paid* .....

charged up like most of the others staying at the hotel.

The tour was supposed to start at 9 o'clock, so we were   **2** ....

getting a little angry and were just about to give in and

go and have a cup of coffee together when the guide   **3** ....

finally turned out at reception 30 minutes late. She   **4** ....

said she had left home on time but had had to go back   **5** ....

as she'd forgotten the tour maps – it came out to be her   **6** ....

first day on the job! First of all, she sorted off which of

us already had maps and which didn't. We eventually   **7** ....

set off more than an hour behind schedule and started   **8** ....

making to the old town. Although there were only about

ten of us, I found it hard to hear her commentary as she   **9** ....

seemed to have singled out the three or four people

closest to her to talk to. As we were walking along I

asked her if we could go and see a beautiful old church,   **10** ....

but she replied rather abruptly that we had to stick in the   **11** ....

itinerary. After that, I decided I'd better write down my   **12** ....

£10 and rely on my own map and intelligence for a more

personal tour of the city.

3 Reported speech

Put the following sentences into reported speech. Use a suitable reporting verb in each case, avoiding *say* if possible. The first one has been done for you.

1 'That's correct. The new ringroad will be built through the wood.'

The government official *confirmed that the new ringroad would be built through the wood.*

2 'Don't worry, I'll repair the back door this weekend.'

Colin 49

3 'All right, it's true. It was me who scratched the car.'

Karen ....

4 'If you don't give me £5,000, I'm going to tell the police all about it.'

Maurice ....

5 'You must come to Dave's party with me on Saturday.'

Hilary ....

6 'Oh by the way, Terry's house is still for sale'.

Silvia ....

7 'Honest to God, I've never seen this money before in my life'.

Mr Penfold ....

8 'Don't go walking in the fog, it can be very dangerous'.

The mountain guide ....

9 'Oh, just a minute, was it Leonardo or Michelangelo who painted the Mona Lisa?'

He couldn't ....

10 'Well, I'd like you all to know Nina and I are getting married next year.'

Julian ....

11 'Oh, I'm easily the best tennis-player at the college.'

Jemima ....

12 'Would you mind repeating the question, Dr McPherson?'

Dr Bianchi ....

13 'The service in this restaurant is incredibly slow.'

George ....

14 'I think it might be better to wait until the manager gets here.'

The shop assistant ....

15 'Well, Jack, if I were you, I'd eat less and take more exercise.'

The doctor ....

STUDY TIP ▶ Reported speech

• When reporting what someone said it is not always necessary to change the tense of what was said if it is still true:

e.g. 'Don't worry, I'm coming next week,' said Gus.

Someone reporting this shortly afterwards would say:

Gus assured us he's coming next week.

4 Formal letters

Look at the advertisement below, which appeared in *The Herald*, and the letter written in response to it. The letter contains **14** mistakes. Find and correct them as in the two examples provided.

COUNTRY COTTAGE HOLIDAYS

Give yourself a break in one of our beautifully restored country cottages with all mod cons – sleeping from 4 to 10 people. Prices from £100 per week.
**Contact: Randolph Jefferies
20 The Green,
Hinton,
Devon HN3 2CC.**

5 Redland Road
Barford BF2 8VR

21st May, 19—

Randolph Jefferies
20 The Green
Hinton
Devon HN3 2CC

Dear Mr Randolf [Jefferies]

I was most interested by [in] your advertisement on 'The Herald' and I am writing for obtain further informations about your country cottage holidays.

In particular, I would like knowing in which parts of the country your cottages are located as my friends and I are interested to stay as far away from large cities as possible. I would like to know too if it would be possible renting a cottage for six people for up to six months and whether pets are allowed as my friends and I have three well-behaved dogs we are planning to take with us.

I should, therefore, be terrible grateful if you will send me full details of your larger more isolated cottages and any brochures you may have.

Thanking you in advance for your help. I look forward to hear from you as early as possible.

Yours faithfully

Sandy Melville

SANDY MELVILLE

5.1 Wordcheck – Holidays

Fill in the missing words in the grid below to reveal another connected word. One is shown as an example.

1   B R O C H U R E
2
3
4
5
6
7
8
9
10
11
12
13

1 Booklet with descriptions and photographs of holiday locations.

2 Person who accompanies and looks after tourists on holiday.

3 Type of accommodation where you do your own cooking.

4 People on holiday often leave one for the waiter.

5 What you send to your friends and family from your holiday location.

6 Typically non-professional photographs taken by people on holiday.

7 Where you can sit and look down on the beach from your hotel room.

8 The place to stay if you're sleeping in a tent.

9 Sunbathers hope to get one without going red!

10 Type of holiday in which everything is paid for before you leave.

11 Going around looking at famous landmarks and monuments.

12 A tourist trip, usually by bus, to go and see something special.

13 Children often make these on the beach.

5.2 Word partners

Match each word in the first column with one in the second column to form a useful word partnership connected with holidays. Look at the example.

1	twin	C	A	break
2	travel	☐	B	bathroom
3	beauty	☐	C	bed
4	hire-	☐	D	resort
5	sea	☐	E	excursions
6	optional	☐	F	company
7	en suite	☐	G	car
8	seaside	☐	H	delicacies
9	annual	☐	I	view
10	seafood	☐	J	spot

Progress Test Two

Units 5 – 8

Check your progress by entering your score in the box at the end of each exercise and at the end of the complete test.

1 Complete the following passage by writing a word or words in each of the numbered spaces.

A summer job

'Oh good, you're here at last. I **(1)** .... what time of day you'd **(2)** .... up,' snapped the boss. 'I **(3)** .... for you since half past eight!'

It was my first day at work and it looked as though I wasn't making a very good start. I apologised and explained that the early morning traffic had been considerably **(4)** .... I'd expected.

'Oh dear! I don't suppose you're used to getting up so early after your easy time at university. To be honest, I'm surprised you were **(5)** .... get here before midday,' he added sarcastically. I smiled and said nothing.

The job was driving a tourist bus around Stratford while Cheryl, the boss's daughter, gave a description of the places of interest we **(6)** .... There were supposed to be a few stops for visits to various places as well.

We **(7)** .... off at half past nine with a bus full of tourists. I **(8)** .... along quite happily when Cheryl poked me in the ribs and hissed, 'How long **(9)** .... your licence? You drive **(10)** .... a complete lunatic! **(11)** .... you drive a bit more slowly, especially when we're going past things I have to talk about.'

'Sorry,' I said, gritting my teeth. 'I **(12)** .... my best.'

At 11 o'clock, we pulled **(13)** .... at Anne Hathaway's cottage. The tourists and Cheryl went inside so I decided to go and have a cup of coffee at a cafe I'd seen just up the road. The cafe was a **(14)** .... further than I realised and I had to stand in the queue for ages – it **(15)** .... taken me at least 20 minutes to get served. By the time I got back to the bus, the tourists and an angry-looking Cheryl **(16)** .... to get back on board.

'Where on earth have you been?' shouted Cheryl.

'I just popped off for a cup of coffee. Your father told me it **(17)** .... OK to go to the cafe near here,' I protested.

'Well, in future, check with me before you go running off.'

'OK, OK,' I said, starting up the bus.

When we got back, Cheryl told her father about my dreadful behaviour. But before he **(18)** .... to open his mouth, I said, 'Look, I've had just about enough of you two. Don't bother to sack me, I **(19)** .... in tomorrow!' and walked out.

I later **(20)** .... out that they had had four different bus drivers in as many weeks!

	20

2 Fill each blank with a suitable form of the word in brackets.

Example: Bridget's terribly *camera-shy* (camera), she never wants to have her photo taken.

1 Maud's .... (eye) got worse as she refused to wear glasses.

2 I'm not used to smoking so a few puffs on a cigarette make me feel quite .... (light).

3 Apparently, eating fish and lots of vegetables greatly increases your life .... (expect).

4 The main .... (draw) of working freelance is the lack of paid holidays.

5 The local TV company was stopping .... (pass) to ask their opinion about the new shopping centre.

6 Low .... (consume) of animal fats generally means a low risk of heart disease.

7 A lot of people keep up their English by listening to radio .... (broad).

8 You'd better read the government .... (guide) on setting up a business abroad.

9 Global warming, or 'the .... (green) effect', is due to a build up of gases in the stratosphere.

10 I was born at home but most babies are born in hospitals .... (now).

10

3 Complete each of the following sentences with the appropriate form of a suitable phrasal verb. An example sentence is provided.

Example: Hal had no trouble in *calling up* all the data we needed on the computer screen.

1 Giving up my job to go and live abroad .... to be the biggest mistake I've ever made.

2 Jane has always .... her brother even when he was accused of murder and everyone else refused to speak to him.

3 This watch used to belong to my great-great-grandfather. It's been .... from father to son for five generations.

4 My karate instructor always .... Robert to demonstrate techniques as he's the best in the class.

5 I've got to drive, so I think I'd better .... orange juice, thanks all the same.

5

4 Match the beginnings of the sentences in column **A** with their endings in column **B** and add the correct particle to complete each phrase. Look at the example provided.

A

1 David is calling a meeting to try and sort ☒ G

2 Can you jot those phone numbers ☐

3 It's a present so could you wrap it ☐

4 Why can't you hang your clothes ☐

5 I saw a very suspicious man hanging ☐

6 We had to prop the table leg ☐

7 They decided to name their little daughter ☐

8 Why don't we check that new pub ☐

9 I couldn't see anything wrong until the doctor pointed it ☐

10 My French is getting a bit rusty so I'm going to brush it ☐

11 I forgot all about the milk and it boiled ☐

B

A .... when you take them off at night?

B .... to me on the X-Ray.

C .... tomorrow evening?

D ....making a terrible mess.

E .... at evening classes.

F .... outside the post office.

G _out_ a misunderstanding with our most important clients.

H .... in some pretty paper?

I .... on a piece of paper . I haven't got a pen.

J .... the doctor who saved her life.

K .... with a pile of old books.

10

5 Choose the best phrase or sentence (given after the text) to fill each of the blanks in the following text. Write one letter (A – H) in each of the numbered spaces. Three of the suggested answers do not fit at all.

Indo-European languages

Today, most European languages and many Asian languages as far east as India are very similar to each other. **(1)** .... about memorising French word lists in school, these so-called 'Indo-European' languages resemble English and each other in terms of vocabulary and grammar, **(2)** .... Only 140 of the modern world's 5,000 tongues belong to this language family, **(3)** .... Thanks to the global expansion of Europeans since 1492 – especially people from England, Spain, Portugal, France and Russia – nearly half the world's present population of five billion now speaks an Indo-European language as its native tongue.

When, however, we go to parts of the world with great linguistic diversity we realise how unusual Europe's linguistic similarity is, and how it calls for explanation. **(4)** ....,in areas of the New Guinea highlands where first contact with the outside world began only in the Twentieth Century, we find languages as different as English is from Chinese being spoken in neighbouring areas. **(5)** .... until some people speaking the mother tongue of the Indo-European language family began to dominate and pushed almost all the other old European languages out of existence.

A   as well as French

B   Eurasia must have originally been as diverse

C   For example

D   which must have originated outside Europe

E   yet differ in this respect from all the world's other languages

F   In spite of this

G   No matter how much we complain

H   but their importance is far out of proportion to their numbers

5

TOTAL

50

Unit 9

1 Relative clauses

Decide if the following sentences, which all contain relative clauses, are punctuated correctly or not. Make any necessary corrections, as in the example.

1 Mark's father, who used to be a diplomat, speaks eight foreign languages.

2 Children, who don't have any brothers or sisters, often find it hard when they first go to school.

3 Have you still got that second-hand computer you bought from that chap you met in the pub we used to go to?

4 The Irish doctor, who used to work at this surgery, has moved to Leeds.

5 Do you remember that little cinema we saw all those old black and white movies at? Well, it's been pulled down!

6 We went to the first performance of the play which turned out to be a complete disaster!

7 It rained all day which meant we couldn't go out at all.

8 DNA which is 98.4% identical in humans and chimpanzees was discovered by Watson and Crick in 1944.

9 The Paris which is in Texas has very little to do with the Paris in France.

10 'Zorro', Mrs Nimmo's favourite cat whose tail was bitten off by a dog isn't very good at balancing any more!

2.1 Phrasal verbs

Complete the following sentences with phrasal verbs from the box below. Use the correct tense or structure. An example is given.

carry out	cut down	cut up	dip into
hold up	make up	spring up	

1 Are all animals' bodies *made up* of cells?

2 Don't forget to .... the potatoes into small pieces before boiling them or they take ages.

3 It's not the sort of book you'd want to read from cover to cover but it's quite interesting to .... now and then.

4 It's a miracle the roof didn't fall in as one of the walls which had been .... it .... suddenly collapsed.

5 Modern computers are capable of .... the most complex operations in micro-seconds.

6 A lot of fast food restaurants have .... in the town centre over the last couple of years.

7 You need fifteen players to .... a rugby team.

8 We had to .... the old oak tree after it was damaged in the storm.

57

2.2 Different meanings

Use a good English/English dictionary to find different uses for the phrasal verbs in the box in **2.1** and complete the sentences, using the right tense. The first one is shown as an example.

1 It took me over an hour to get *made up* for the part of Othello.

2 If you want to lose weight, you should .... on the amount of dairy products you eat.

3 He .... some story about catching the wrong train to explain his lateness.

4 Joe and Sally are always having quarrels but they always .... in the end.

5 The start of the concert was .... by the late arrival of the group.

6 I can't afford a summer holiday this year unless I .... my savings.

7 Three masked men tried to .... the security van last week.

8 Monty accidentally trod on the rake, which .... and hit him on the nose!

3 Quantifiers – each/every, either/neither etc.

Correct any incorrect uses of quantifiers in the following sentences. The first one is shown as an example.

1 None the supermarkets in our town sells fresh fish.
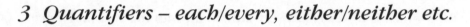

2 Our two children are very alike; everyone has red hair and green eyes.

3 Which of these two umbrellas is yours? None.

4 How much are these second-hand books? £1 every one.

5 You can go either way at the fork in the road; they all lead to the beach.

6 Is Phyllis a nurse or a dentist? Neither. She's a psychiatrist.

7 Each record in her collection was by the same group!

8 We asked a young couple for directions but none of them knew where the street was.

9 I've seen all Meryl Streep's films and she's brilliant in every one.

10 Each tyre on the car had been deliberately slashed by vandals.

> ## STUDY TIP ▶ Both and all
>
> • These are placed after auxiliary verbs but before main verbs:
>
> e.g. They can **both/all** swim.
> Do you **both/all** speak French?
> They have **both/all** been to New Zealand.
> We **both/all** have black tea for breakfast.

4 Linking and logical devices – Cause and result, purpose and time

Complete the following sentences with suitable linking devices. An asterisk (*) indicates at least two possible answers. Look at the example provided.

1 It was necessary to use a microscope *in order to/so as to/to establish the existence of organisms in the drinking water.

2 They got to the shop at 6 a.m. *..they would be able to get the best bargains in the sale.

3 You'd better take your cheque book with you .... it costs more than you expect.

4 The apple crop this year has been terrible *.. the unseasonal frosts we had in May.

5 *.. there was a train strike, we had to spend an extra two days in Otranto.

6 The man was .... rude .... the manager had to ask him to leave the restaurant.

7 Vince didn't get to bed until 5 a.m. .... he's feeling exhausted this morning.

8 Erica's new boss turned out to be .... a tyrant .... she resigned after a week!

9 The new model is slightly larger and *.. more expensive.

10 *.. you arrive in Bombay, give us a call to let us know everything's OK.

11 We won't be able to forward the goods .... we receive your cheque.

12 .... I had the chance to reverse into the parking space someone else drove straight into it.

13 *..................................... had I dropped off to sleep .... next door's dog started howling at the moon.

14 .... he ate all the sandwiches. *.. he drank all the wine. .... he collapsed on the sofa!

15 .... Steve was upstairs having a shower, the burglars were downstairs helping themselves to his stereo, computer and TV.

5 Dictionary skills

In each of the following exercises you should use a good English/English dictionary to help you find the answers.

A   Opposites – prefixes

Find the opposites for the following words using the prefixes in the bubble below. The first one has been done for you.

> dis–   il–   im–   in–   ir–   mis–   non–   un–

1 formal	informal	9 soluble	....
2 mobile	....	10 behave	....
3 rational	....	11 logical	....
4 comfortable	....	12 comfort	....
5 smoker	....	13 spell	....
6 relevant	....	14 polite	....
7 reliable	....	15 legible	....
8 respect	....	16 resident	....

STUDY TIP ▶   **Negative prefixes**

- Record in groups those words that start with the same negative prefix:

e.g. (verbs) misbehave, misinform, mislay
(adjectives) misguided, misnamed

- Remember that certain prefixes occur before certain spellings:

e.g. *il–* (illogical, illiterate) – usually before a word beginning with *l*
im– (impersonal, immature) – usually before a word beginning with *m* or *p*
ir– (irrational, irreparable) – usually before a word beginning with *r*

B Synonyms and antonyms

Write a (near) synonym and antonym for each of the following adjectives.

	SYNONYM	ANTONYM
17 cheeky	....	....
18 brainy	....	....
19 skinny	....	....
20 handy	....	....

6 Formal letters

The following letter is in response to the job advertisement shown below. Complete the letter with suitable words or phrases. Look at the example.

DESK EDITOR

CIRCA £13,500 p.a.

An experienced editor is required by an expanding publisher of books on leisure, craft and wood-related subjects. The position involves taking charge of the day-to-day process of producing highly illustrated books from receipt of manuscript to approval for press. A practical approach is needed, with good keyboard and organisational skills, as well as the ability to work quickly and accurately to tight deadlines.

You will need to be able to work independently, although you will be part of a small team, and to be concerned with maintaining the highest standards.

Please apply in writing to:

Mr A E Phillips, Publisher
GMC Publications
166 High Street, Lewes, East Sussex BN7 1XU

---

34 St Mary's Way
Buxton
Derbyshire BU4 8JS

(1) 14th October 19—

Mr A E Phillips
GMC Publications
(2) ....
Lewes
East Sussex BN7 1XU

Dear Mr Phillips

I am interested (3)................................. for the (4).............................. desk editor which (5)............................... in 'The Independent' yesterday.

(6)................................. applying is that I (7)................................. for 10 years as an assistant editor in a small publishing company concerned mainly with books on leisure and hobbies and I am now (8)................................. a post which would (9).............................. more responsibility and independence to make editorial and organisational decisions.

I am used to and enjoy the challenge (10) .... to tight deadlines to produce high quality books. I have fast and accurate keyboard skills and am familiar with all modern publishing computer software.

I would be able (11) .... interview at any time which is (12) .... to you.

(13) ....

(14) ....

Olivia James

(15) ....

7 Wordcheck – The Environment

Complete the missing words in the following sentences. The first one is shown as an example.

1 Emissions from factories and traffic exhaust are responsible for much of the *pollution* in the air we breathe.

2 Fossil f .... , such as coal and oil, cannot last forever.

3 If more people started r .... paper and other waste, we would not need to destroy so many forests.

4 Clearing rainforests leads to d .... because the rain that falls runs away, which means there's no evaporation and no further rain.

5 Unfortunately, tropical t .... , such as mahogany, is one of the Third World's highest earning exports.

6 Most people don't realise that the b .... they use to clean their bathroom with goes on to poison animals and plants in rivers.

7 Many of the products we buy in supermarkets are wrapped up in totally unnecessary p .... to make them appear more attractive.

8 Rainforests absorb carbon dioxide and slow down global warming which is caused by the so-called g .... effect.

Unit 10

1 Past perfect

In the following passage fill in the spaces with an appropriate form of the past simple, past continuous, past perfect simple or past perfect continuous of the verb in brackets. The first one has been done for you.

Frogs in my car

1 **(1)** had been waiting (wait) for over an hour when Barry finally
(2) .... (turn up) on the tractor. He
(3) .... (explain) he **(4)** .... (hold up)
by a fallen tree in the road. I **(5)** .... (not find) this hard
to believe as a gale force wind **(6)** .... (blow) for the past
five hours accompanied by torrential rain. The reason why I
(7) .... (call) Barry was that my car
(8) .... (lie) on its side in a ditch. I
(9) .... (drive) along very slowly in the terrible weather
when suddenly a large dog **(10)** .... (appear) in front of
me. I **(11)** .... (brake) to avoid hitting it and the car
(12) .... (skid) out of control on the water and mud on
the road and went into the ditch. I **(13)** .... (manage) to
get out through the window. The problem now was that the car
(14) .... (fill up) with water and mud!

    Within seconds Barry, who **(15)** .... (wear) enormous
rubber boots, **(16)** .... (tie) a rope to the front bumper
of the car and **(17)** .... (pull) it out with the tractor. After
a few minutes the car was the right way up and back on the road again.
We **(18)** .... (open) the door and out
(19) .... (jump) two big frogs which
(20) .... (swim) in through the open window!

STUDY TIP ▶ Past perfect tense

- Remember this tense is not used very frequently in English.

- It is not used when the time conjunctions *before* and *after* make the order of events clear.

e.g. Before they went on holiday, they had ~~had~~ seven vaccinations.

- It is used with *by the time that* and *when*:

e.g. By the time ⎫
     When   ⎬ they went on holiday, they had had seven vaccinations.

2.1 Conditional 3

In the following sentences, put the verbs in brackets in the correct tense to form 3rd or mixed conditionals. Put any other words in brackets in the correct place. An example is given.

1 If I hadn't seen (not see) it with my own eyes, I wouldn't have believed (not believe) it!

2 We .... (still live) in Cardiff if we .... (not find) someone to buy our house last year.

3 If Hilary .... (not look) out of the window at that moment, she .... (not spot) the criminals trying to break into her car.

4 Nobody .... (ever guess) he was a thief if he .... (not catch) red-handed taking money from the safe.

5 Henry .... (not ever get) that job at the bank if he .... (not go) to school with the manager's son.

6 Just think, if I .... (take) that job with the export/import company, I .... (live) in Sao Paulo now, not Manchester!

7 If the doctor .... (not notice) the defect when I was a child, I .... (be) practically blind by now.

8 We .... (be) home in bed ages ago if you .... (not lose) the map!

9 Frank .... (not be) here today if that boy .... (not know) how to do artificial respiration.

10 If you .... (listen) to the traffic report on the radio this morning, we .... (not sit) here in this jam!

2.2 1st, 2nd, 3rd and mixed conditionals

Rewrite the following sentences as conditionals. The first one is shown as an example.

1 Eric was with us so we didn't get lost.

   If Eric hadn't been with us, we'd have got lost.

2 We got soaking wet on Sunday and now we've all got colds.

   If ....

3 I'm afraid I don't know so I can't tell you.

   If ....

4 The weather could be bad on Saturday, in which case we'll have to cancel the barbecue.

   We ....

5 I'm living in Italy because I got married to an Italian.

   I ....

6 Sorry I didn't phone you but I lost the bit of paper with your number on.

....

7 We don't get on very well because she's so aggressive.

If ....

8 We've got a broken window because you and your friends were playing football in the back yard!

We ....

9 I missed the end of the film so I don't know who the murderer was.

If ....

10 Jimmie's father might buy him a new bike; it depends on him passing his exams.

If ....

11 As we'd already seen the film we didn't go to the cinema.

We ....

12 Zoe tripped and fell just as she was about to win the race.

Zoe ....

STUDY TIP ➤ Conditionals

- Each conditional has a more formal equivalent:

Type 1: If you arrive late, go straight to my office.
Should you arrive late, go straight to my office.

Type 2: If we reduced the price, we'd make no profit.
Were we to reduce the price, we'd make no profit.
(N.B. This is a very uncommon form.)

Type 3: If she had phoned, I would have met her.
Had she phoned, I would have met her.

3.1 Phrasal verbs

Complete the following sentences with phrasal verbs from the box below. Use the right tense or structure. The first one is shown as an example.

| break out | bring out | cut off | get over | put down to | put out |

1 Quick action by the police prevented fighting from breaking out between rival groups of fans after the football match.

2 Sports commentators have .... her poor performance .... lack of training.

3 The magazine article .... the more unpleasant side to the actor's personality.

4 The gas supply was .... for about four hours as they had to repair some leaking pipes.

5 Herbie asked them to ....their cigarettes as he is allergic to smoke.

6 As Consuelo didn't speak any English, it was rather difficult for her to .... what she wanted us to do.

7 In the Middle Ages, there was very little you could do if a smallpox epidemic ....near your home.

8 I phoned to let them know which plane I'd be on but I was...............
.... before I could tell them.

3.2   Different meanings

Use a good English/English dictionary to find different uses for the phrasal verbs in the box in **3.1**. The first one has been done for you.

1 I hear FIAT have brought out a new model but I haven't seen it yet.

2 I know they split up over three years ago but he's never really ....
.... her.

3 Jack shouldn't have spent so much time and money on the publicity campaign – still, he'll just have to ....it ....
experience.

4 He looked a bit different last time I saw him, maybe because he'd .... his ponytail ....

5 She .... the problem of lack of time by hiring a house-cleaner.

6 The prison is supposed to be high security but twelve prisoners ....
...............last month.

7 The radio station ....a warning about the severe weather only minutes before it arrived!

8 She's an exceptional teacher. She .... the best in all her pupils.

4 Instructions

Convert the information in the formal instructions on page **67** into an informal version, which has been started for you. Use some of the phrases in the bubble below.

> Next/Then/After that ...   Once/When you've done that ...
>
> Remember to ...   Last(ly)/Finally ...
>
> Be careful (not) to ...   Don't ...   Don't forget to ...

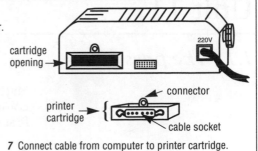

INSTALLATION OF PRINTER CARTRIDGE
1 Ensure that power is off in both computer and printer.
2 Locate cartridge opening in back of printer.
3 Ensure all packaging etc. has been removed from cartridge opening.
4 Insert cartridge into the opening with cable socket facing outwards.
5 Slide cartridge in without using force until you hear a click.
6 Providing the connector is fitted in its socket, tighten the screw easily.

7 Connect cable from computer to printer cartridge.

Here's how to put in the printer cartridge:

First of all, make sure you've switched off the computer and the printer.

Then ....

....

....

....

....

....

5 *Wordcheck – Fire*

There are **18** words connected with fire and fire fighting in the box below. You will find **6** horizontally, **8** vertically and **4** diagonally. Three have been found for you.

C	R	T	A	S	P	A	R	K	S	T	U	R
F	O	E	Y	M	D	E	M	B	E	R	S	E
U	R	N	B	O	I	X	A	R	L	B	O	S
H	A	G	F	U	B	T	P	I	N	A	T	C
O	V	I	L	L	R	I	F	G	E	L	Z	U
S	I	N	E	D	A	N	T	A	N	A	G	E
E	B	E	D	E	F	G	L	D	N	R	O	F
K	S	P	V	R	A	U	R	E	T	M	B	I
A	M	C	F	M	H	I	O	A	X	C	E	R
E	F	L	A	M	E	S	O	M	T	L	S	E
W	I	G	U	P	N	H	E	A	T	I	R	M
I	S	M	O	K	E	E	K	T	O	L	O	A
H	U	T	Y	S	A	R	S	O	N	T	A	N

Unit 11

1.1 The passive

Match up the beginning of each sentence in column **A** with its ending in column **B** and add a suitable passive verb form in the space provided. The first one is shown as an example.

A

1 In the past, small amounts of cocaine *used to be used*. ☐ⓖ

2 Salt .... on roads ☐

3 Central heating .... ☐

4 In the future, many of today's hereditary diseases .... ☐

5 Not so long ago, teeth .... ☐

6 In my grandfather's time, a driving licence .... ☐

7 Undeveloped film .... ☐

8 150 years ago, Gaelic .... ☐

9 'Graded readers' are books in which the language .... ☐

10 Hand gestures .... ☐

11 The world's tropical rainforests .... ☐

12 In India, cows .... ☐

B

A to mean different things in different countries.

B to direct sunlight.

C much more widely in Scotland than it is today.

D by the Romans.

E so quickly that they may all have gone by 2035!

F when there is snow and ice.

G in the production of Coca-cola.

H as sacred animals.

I at a post office without having to take a test!

J without any anaesthetic!

K so that learners can read them more easily.

L through genetic engineering.

1.2 Fill in the gaps

Complete the gaps in the following passage by putting the verbs in brackets into an appropriate passive form. You will also have to put any other words in brackets in the correct place. Look at the example given.

Well, last month most of the lambs **(1)** *were sold* (sell) at the market, although we've still got ten, which **(2)** .... (probably send) next week. When all the lambs have gone, the sheep **(3)**...............................(take) to another part of the farm. After that, we usually start on the fruit, although the blackcurrants **(4)** .... (already pick) because it was an early season this year. The plums can't **(5)** .... (pick) for another three weeks by law as they **(6)** .... (spray) only seven weeks ago. Of course, they still have **(7)**...............................(gather) by hand, unlike the blackcurrants, which **(8)** .... (harvest) by machine nowadays. The plums and blackcurrants **(9)** .... (both make) into jam and preserve. Then we have what's called the 'bag fruit', which is apples and pears. Since the fruit doesn't have to be in good condition **(10)** .... (make) into cider and perry, it **(11)** .... (treat) pretty badly. For example, there are no skilled pickers involved, the trees **(12)**...............................(just shake) until the fruit drops to the ground, where it **(13)**............................... (collect) and **(14)** .... (put) into bags. As you can imagine, handling the bags is a very dirty job as the juice leaks out everywhere. But I hope the whole process **(15)** .... (automate) before much longer.

2 The … the … – comparatives

Complete the following sentences with a suitable comparative form. The first one is shown as an example.

1 The *hotter* (hot) the curry, the *better* (good) she likes it!

2 The .... (interesting) the book, the .... (likely) I am to try and finish it in one evening!

3 The .... (easy) a job is to do, the .... (highly) paid are the people who do it.

4 The .... (wine) he drank, the .... (clearly) he spoke.

5 The .... (close) it got to the time of the interview, the ....she became.

6 The ....(humid) it became, the ....they felt.

7 The .... (far) we climbed up the mountain, the .... the clouds became.

8 .... , the more determined I am to succeed.

9 The less students contribute in class, ...·

10 .... , the less fluently one speaks a foreign language.

3 Phrasal verbs

Complete the following sentences with a suitable phrasal verb from the box below. Remember to use the correct tense or grammatical structure. The first one has been done for you.

face up to	pick out	tune in	work out	fall back on	tick off
put down	eke out	steer away from		fight out	

1 Don't forget to *tune in* tomorrow at 8.15 to find out who killed Lady Redfern in the last episode of our Radio Murder Mystery series.

2 When packing, I always make a check-list so I can .... things .... as I put them in the suitcase.

3 I think it would be best if you .... your complaints in a letter addressed to the manager.

4 They'll eventually have to.............. .... the fact that the company is going to be closed down.

5 It is said that Isaac Newton .... the law of gravity after he'd been hit on the head by an apple!

6 I try and .... talking about politics with Steven but he always gets back to it sooner or later.

7 When I was a student, I .... what little money I had by buying only second-hand clothes.

8 There's only one place left and I'm not deciding who should have it. You'll have to .... it .... amongst yourselves.

9 When we both lost our jobs at the same time, it was lucky we had our savings to ....

10 The old lady had no trouble in .... the thief at the identity parade.

4 Make/cause etc.

Add a suitable ending to each of the following sentences using an infinitive verb form with or without *to*. Look at the example provided.

1 Reading an article about the 'greenhouse effect' persuaded Gary *to travel by bicycle more frequently.*

2 The lack of rain caused most of the plants ....
....

3 The park-keeper wouldn't let the children ....
....

4 Driving while under the influence of alcohol causes people...................
....

5 The TV pictures of the damage caused by the flood made us all ....
....

6 What the doctor said about lung cancer and heart disease convinced Moyra ....
....

7 The customs officer asked Boris ....
....

8 The examination invigilator didn't let anyone ....
....

9 Living and working in a foreign country usually forces you ....
....

10 Having to deal with tiresome bureaucracy makes me ....
....

> ## STUDY TIP ▶ Make
>
> - Remember that when *make* is used passively it takes *to* before a following verb:
>
> e.g. They made her leave the room.
>   She was made **to** leave the room.

5 Informal letters

Use the following notes to write a letter of invitation to a friend. You must use all the words in the same order as the notes. You may add words and change the form of words where necessary but do not add any extra information. The first one has been done for you.

1 many thanks postcard Greece – get last week.

2 glad hear have good time – apart sunburn!

3 hope get over it – feel better now.

4 anyway reason write – Kim and I party Saturday 19th celebrate end exams.

5 know rather long way come but wonder you like stay whole weekend.

6 both hope able make it.

7 can let know come by next Friday?

8 Hope hear soon

Dear Sam,

1 Many thanks for your postcard from *Greece*, which we got last week.

2 ....

3 ....

4 ....

5 ....

6 ....

7 ....

8 ....

All the best,

STUDY TIP ▶ Informal letters

• Remember the following points when writing an informal letter:

DO	DON'T
write the salutation (e.g. Dear Sally) against the left hand margin.	begin *Dear Friend*
begin the first paragraph under the first letter of the correspondent's name.	
indent the following paragraphs slightly in from the left hand margin.	
end with *Best wishes* or *Love* (depending on how well you know the person).	use the formal endings *Yours sincerely/faithfully*.

---

6 Wordcheck – Character and personality

In each of the following groups of words there is one that doesn't fit. Underline the odd word out. The first one has been done for you.

1	critical	defensive	sarcastic	<u>persistent</u>
2	keen	restless	eager	ambitious
3	harsh	unfeeling	impatient	insensitive
4	diligent	talkative	friendly	chatty
5	shy	withdrawn	timid	calm
6	carefree	attentive	careful	cautious
7	happy	content	cheerful	charming
8	trustworthy	dynamic	reliable	dependable

Progress Test Three

Units 9 – 11

Check your progress by entering your score in the box at the end of each exercise and at the end of the complete test.

1 Complete the following passage by writing a word or words in each of the numbered spaces.

A mountain excursion

My friend Nigel, **(1)** .... had just completed an advanced orienteering course, had somehow **(2)** .... me to go on an excursion across the mountains with him. When we set out just after lunch, it had been clear and sunny but for the past hour or so it **(3)** .... foggier and foggier. We had been walking along under a blanket of thick fog for about half an hour **(4)** .... Nigel suddenly announced we were lost!

'Oh, that's marvellous!' I said. 'You **(5)** .... me come on this stupid hike up a mountain in the fog and now you tell me we're lost! I thought you knew how to read a map.'

'I do,' protested Nigel. 'It's just that all the landmarks **(6)** .... by this fog and it's hardly my fault that you dropped the compass into that river, is it? If you hadn't lost that, at least we **(7)** .... which direction we were going in. We'll have to find somewhere to spend the night,' he added ominously.

We walked on a little way **(8)** ....we came up against an old stone wall **(9)** .... seemed to be part of an old farmhouse that I supposed **(10)** .... by its former occupants.

'Well, it looks like survival tactics from now on,' said Nigel, apparently enjoying the idea. 'The **(11)** .... it gets, the better I like it,' he added with a grin, **(12)** .... me to wonder if he wasn't getting a little overexcited.

'Right, **(13)** .... I go and get some wood **(14)** .... a fire with, you stay here and unpack the survival kit from my rucksack', ordered Nigel as he disappeared into the fog.

(15) .... about ten minutes, he came back with an armful of sticks which appeared **(16)** .... cut into convenient lengths and left on the mountain.

'OK. I'm going to try and fix up a shelter. In the **(17)** ...., you get a fire started,' he barked.

(18) .... had I got the fire started than I heard a movement. I turned round to see a little old lady looking at me furiously. 'For goodness sake put that wood back, I need it **(19)** .... the fence with.'

Apparently, we had wandered up to the back wall of her garden. If Nigel hadn't ordered me to light a fire, we **(20)** .... a miserable night in the fog only minutes away from civilisation!

20

73

2 Fill each blank with a suitable form of the word in brackets.

Example: People should take certain fire *prevention* (prevent) measures.

1 Eddie just can't stop working and relax any more, he's turning into a real .... (work).

2 .... (content) people are often critical and sarcastic.

3 Tests have shown that people's blood pressure goes up when they are in red coloured .... (surround).

4 Insecure people often do things just to avoid other people's .... (approve).

5 Most of us think we have a rational and well-balanced .... (look) on life.

6 There has been a .... (miracle) increase in recovery from leukaemia in the last 30 years.

7 Faulty electrical .... (apply) are a relatively common cause of fires in offices, factories and hotels.

8 Without colour dyes people would find a lot of processed food rather .... (appetite).

9 Because he said so little in meetings, his colleagues thought he was .... (commit) to his work, but actually he was just timid.

10 Some hardwood is produced on .... (plant) so that natural forests are not destroyed.

10

3 Complete each of the following sentences with the appropriate form of a suitable phrasal verb. An example is provided.

Example: I enjoy *dipping into* the encyclopaedia from time to time.

1 Sheila .... her duties efficiently enough but she's not really interested in her job.

2 When I woke up, everyone else had gone to bed and the fire had

.... , leaving me shivering in the cold, damp room.

3 We were on holiday there when the civil war ....

4 Don't forget to .... your job application before this Friday. The address is in yesterday's paper.

5 There was so much snow that our village was completely .... and food had to be brought in by helicopter.

5

4 In most of the lines of the following text there is a mistake connected with the verbs (tense, form, agreement, etc.). Underline each mistake and write the correct verb form in the space at the end of the line. If there is no mistake in a line, put a tick (✔) in the space. See the examples provided.

Solving the elk problem

Motorists who find themselves driving along the lonely roads	e.g.	✔
through Sweden's extensive pine forests <u>were</u> more relaxed these	e.g.	*are*
days. Small plastic bottles which are been hung from roadside	1	....
trees had calmed their deepest fear – colliding with an elk!	2	....
Each bottle contain a pungent blend of animal fat and wolf's	3	....
urine. The idea is simple – because wolves are hunting elks	4	....
the smell makes the elks to avoid the roads like the plague.	5	....
'It really works, we're very excited about it,' said spokesman	6	....
Lars Olofson, added that 25,000 accidents are caused	7	....
by elks every year, according to research he's just completed.	8	....
The cost of protecting the roads will have been cut by the new	9	....
potion, which cost only 2 krona per metre compared with 40	10	....
krona per metre for the traditional metal fences used before.	11	....
The wolf cocktail had been invented two years ago by Mr	12	....
Olofson's father, who used it to stop elks to eat his onions.	13	....
'It's a top-secret formula,' added Lars, 'if everyone started	14	....
using it, the elks would soon have become desensitised to it.'	15	....

15

TOTAL

50

Unit 12

1 Modal verbs

Complete the following sentences using a suitable modal verb to express obligation or permission together with the verb in brackets. The first one is shown as an example.

1 You *must go* (go) and see that new play at the Adelphi. It's marvellous!

2 Guests .... (leave) their valuables in the hotel safe if they wish.

3 It was lucky we .... (change) any money as all the banks were shut.

4 We .... (rush) after all. The plane was over an hour late taking off.

5 You .... (have) a special licence to drive lorries weighing over two tons.

6 Sorry to interrupt, Professor Cripwell, ... I .... (ask) you a quick question?

7 In the future, European citizens .... (travel) from one country to another inside Europe without going through customs.

8 We really .... (have) the car washed. It's absolutely filthy!

9 I've no idea where the inn is. So when we get to the village, we .... (ask) for directions.

10 Unlike many other countries, young men in Britain .... (do) compulsory military service as it was abolished in 1957.

11 You used .... (build) a house more or less anywhere on your own land 100 years ago. Today you ....:.. (put) a shed in your garden without planning permission!

12 .... we .... (discuss) this any further? I'm sure we've all got a good idea of the problem now.

13 You .... (keep) the receipt. They won't take it back without one now.

14 I hope we .... (build) an extension on the back of our house next year.

15 At my last job, we .... (make) any personal phone calls from the office. We .... (use) the public call box in the street!

2 Collocations

Complete the following sentences to make common word partnerships, or collocations. The first one has been done for you.

1 William *takes* himself rather seriously, I'm afraid.

2 The government broke their .... not to put up taxes.

3 The town council plans to.................. a public meeting to discuss the new car park.

4 Thomas wasted a lot of money on ineffectual advertisements but, in the end, he just put it down to...................

5 Kevin's always cracking terrible.................. that only he laughs at!

6 A break from the everyday routine................... everyone a lot of good.

7 Laura raised an interesting................... at the staff meeting yesterday.

8 Jo was asked to................... an explanation for her extraordinary behaviour.

9 The doctor tried to put me at my................... about the operation but I couldn't help being worried.

10 The consultant advised us to bring our computer system up to..................., describing what we've got as antiquated and practically obsolete!

11 The manager told us to give.................. to the publicity campaign as that was the most important thing to get finished.

12 She was trying to................... him a compliment but it came out all wrong.

13 Amanda................... an excuse about visiting a sick friend but I don't think she really wanted to come.

14 I made a real................... when I asked her about her husband. How was I to know they'd just split up?

15 It was getting very late but nobody seemed to want to make a................... to break up the party.

STUDY TIP ▶ Collocations

- It is very important to know which words frequently go together to form collocations (word partnerships). A good idea to help build up your knowledge of collocations is to create 'key word grids':

e.g.

VERBS	DESCRIBING WORDS	KEY WORD	WORDS THAT COME AFTER
catch	wrong		stop
miss	last	BUS	pass
get on	crowded		fare
stop	night		station

- Try to make your own grids with common key words.

STUDY TIP ▶ Phonetics

- Some phonetic symbols are quite easy to understand e.g. /k/, /z/, /p/ but there are a few which need to be learnt. Do you know what sounds these symbols represent? If not, check in a dictionary.

  /ɔː/ /θ/ /dʒ/ /ð/ /ɜː/ /tʃ/

3 Dictionary skills

In all of the following exercises you should use a good English/English dictionary to help you find the answers.

A Phonetics

Find the pronunciation key at the beginning or end of your dictionary. Use it to help you match the following words with the vowel sound they contain. Write the correct phonetic symbol in the box after each word.

words		sounds
1 cut	☐	/uː/
2 caught	☐	/æ/
3 kit	☐	/ɔː/
4 cat	☐	/ɜː/
5 cot	☐	/ɑː/
6 curt	☐	/ʌ/
7 coot	☐	/ɪ/
8 cart	☐	/ɒ/

B Spelling vs. pronunciation

Similar spelling does not always mean similar pronunciation in English. Decide if the following pairs of words have the same vowel sound. Write **S** (same) or **D** (different) in the box.

9 bomb	comb	☐
10 low	tow	☐
11 weight	eight	☐
12 stove	glove	☐
13 pour	sour	☐
14 laughter	daughter	☐
15 food	mood	☐
16 rear	pear	☐
17 none	done	☐
18 mown	town	☐

C Pronunciation

The combination of letters *ough* can be pronounced in seven different ways in English. Put the words in the bubble below in the correct list depending on the pronunciation of *ough*.

> nought   through   trough   rough   thorough
>
> though   tough   borough   enough   bough
>
> drought   thought   cough   plough   dough

	/ʌf/	/ə/	/aʊ/	/əʊ/
e.g.	bl<u>uff</u>	<u>a</u>gain	h<u>ow</u>	n<u>o</u>
	....	....	....	....
	....	....	....	....
	....	....	....	....

	/ɔː/	/ɒf/	/uː/
	s<u>aw</u>	c<u>o</u>ffee	t<u>oo</u>
	....	....	....
	....	....	....
	....	....	....

4 Formal letters

The sentences below come from two different letters. **1**) Mark each sentence **A** or **B** to show which letter it comes from. **2**) Put the sentences in the correct order by numbering them. **3**) Complete the two letters adding any missing words and creating paragraphs where necessary. You will also need to add the appropriate salutations. Look at the example.

a I, however, wrote down 5 p.m. in my diary. B

b The increased revenue from cigarette sales could then be spent on a sustained publicity campaign to.................... smokers to give up.

c I look forward to hearing from you at your .... convenience.

d This was .... to an unfortunate misunderstanding between my secretary and myself regarding the time of the meeting.

e I would like to .... to the letter written by Mr D Fenton regarding cigarettes and advertising which .... in Monday's edition of your newspaper.

f I am .... sorry to have .... your time like this and am most anxious to arrange a time for another meeting as soon as possible.

g First and foremost, I would like to point .... that in Britain the annual death rate from lung cancer per 100,000 of the population is 10 among non-smokers, rising to 251 among those smoking 25 cigarettes a day.

h I .... you that there will be no misunderstanding over the time in the future.

i It.................... to me that such statistics provide a very clear case for .... increasing taxes on cigarettes and completely banning all forms of advertising.

j Quite simply, my secretary told me, correctly, that the meeting was at 15.00 hours.

k I am writing to .... for not attending the meeting on Tuesday afternoon.

A

> Science and Information
> British Medical Association
> London WC1
>
> 12th April, 19—
>
> The Editor
> The Independent
> City Road
> London EC1
>
> Dear Sir,
>
>
> *Katherine Hedge*
>
> Dr Katherine Hedge

B

Oxford Caterers Ltd
20 High Street
Oxford OX2

21st May, 19—

Mrs H A Barns
Cotswold Hotel
Cheltenham GL10

Dear Mrs Barns,

L.T.Lamb

Larry T Lamb

5 Wordcheck – Customs and behaviour

Fill in the missing words in the grid below to reveal another word connected with the topic. The first one is shown as an example.

```
1              E T I Q U E T T E
2                _ _ _ _ _ _
3                _ _ _
4        _ _ _ _ _ _ _
5                _ _ _ _ _ _ _
6          _ _ _ _ _ _ _ _
7                _ _ _ _ _ _ _
8    _ _ _ _ _ _ _ _ _
9          _ _ _ _ _ _ _ _ _ _
10 _ _ _ _ _ _ _ _ _ _
11        _ _ _ _
12        _ _ _ _ _ _
13 _ _ _ _ _ _ _
```

1 Customs and rules for polite behaviour.

2 On meeting, some people take each other in their arms, or ....

3 Bend the head or body as a sign of respect or greeting.

4 How you might feel if someone behaves too formally or too informally.

5 Synonym for 'impoliteness'.

6 Try and make a good one when you meet someone for the first time.

7 It's best to offer one if number **11** happens to you.

8 If you are rude to someone, you show them ....

9 Friendly and welcoming entertainment of guests or strangers.

10 A remark intended to show admiration or approval.

11 You may accidentally do this to someone by breaking conventions of behaviour from another culture.

12 If you have good ...., you behave and speak very politely.

13 Synonym for 'behaviour'.

Unit 13

1 Past tenses for hypothetical situations

Complete the sentences to express your thoughts for each of the following situations. Look at the example given.

1 Your dream is to be able to surf.

I **wish** I could surf!

2 Your colleague keeps interrupting you when you're speaking.

I'd rather you ....

3 It's ten to nine and your sister has to be at the station by nine!

Come on, it's time you ....

4 You lost your temper at work this morning and now you're sorry.

If only I ....

5 Your brother is pretending not to have seen his old girlfriend.

Why are you acting as though ....?

6 You think your friend might lose his job and he should think about this possibility.

But suppose you ....

7 A friend has rather stupidly given your phone number to an insurance agent.

I'd rather you ....

8 Someone who's rather wealthy is always complaining about having no money.

Oh, stop talking as if you ....

9 You're depressed because you have to go back to work tomorrow.

If only I ....

10 A passenger on a boat stopped you from falling overboard by holding on to your belt!

If he ....

11 You dream of being rich and travelling round the world in your own plane.

If I ....

12 You think you may have called your friend at an inconvenient moment.

Would you rather I ....?

STUDY TIP ▷ **Past for hypothetical situations**

- Remember that in English we use past tenses to talk about an imaginary action or state which isn't true/isn't happening or wasn't true/didn't happen:

e.g. I wish she was happy. = she's not happy at the moment
If only she'd studied for the exam. = she didn't study

83

2 Dictionary skills

In all of the following exercises you should use a good English/English dictionary to help you find the answers.

A Collocations (word partners)

Some of the following sentences, which contain actions and parts of the body you do them with, are incorrect. Correct any mistakes, as in the example.

1 Please stop drumming your *fingers* ~~thumbs~~ on the table – it's driving me mad!

2 Steve screwed his face up in pain when he accidentally banged his head on the low doorway.

3 The station guard shrugged his arms unhelpfully when I asked him where the nearest bank was.

4 I couldn't help clapping my palms with joy when I heard I'd finally passed my driving test.

5 Billy's such a spoilt child – if he doesn't get his own way he stamps his legs and screams until you give in.

6 The old woman shook her fist at the children stealing apples from her garden.

7 Everyone nodded their necks in agreement at the director's proposal for increasing sales.

8 I cupped my hands and drank greedily from the mountain stream.

B Metaphors and idioms

Match up the beginnings and endings of the following sentences and add a word from the bubble below to make a suitable metaphor or idiom.

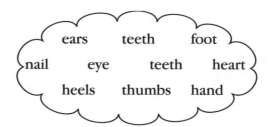

> ears teeth foot
> nail eye teeth heart
> heels thumbs hand

9 Sally's prepared to fight tooth and .... ☐	A but we just caught it by the skin of our ....
10 I really put my................... in it ☐	B to keep possession of her house.
11 When I was at school ☐	C when the police asked him about his movements last Friday evening.
12 The debate got completely out of .... ☐	D I tried to learn Shakespeare's sonnets by ....
13 The train was about to leave as we got to the station ☐	E she's head over .... in love with him.
14 It's no good warning Judy about Harry; ☐	F I'm up to my................... in work.
15 I keep dropping things today; ☐	G I've got to go to the toilet for a minute.

16 Robin lied through his .... ☐

17 Can you keep an .... on my luggage, ☐

18 Sorry, but I just can't make it to the dinner party; ☐

H I seem to be all fingers and ....

I when I asked her about her job – she's been sacked!

J when two old ladies started hitting each other with their handbags.

STUDY TIP ▷ Learning idioms and metaphors

- A good way to remember an idiom or a metaphor is to draw a picture of it (it doesn't have to be very good) – this will help you remember better than simply writing it down! Use the 4-column method shown below.

PICTURE	FIRST LETTERS	IDIOM	EXAMPLE SENTENCE
	k.... a.... e.... o....	keep an eye on	Could you keep an eye on my bag while I go to the toilet?
	o.... t.... b....	have something on the brain	Robert must have golf on the brain – he never stops talking about it!

- Once you have created this grid, you can test yourself by covering everything except the pictures with a piece of paper to see if you can remember. If you can't, slide the piece of paper to the right to reveal the first letters. Try it, it works.

---

3 Directions

Complete the following directions based on the sketch map shown below. Put only one word in each space. The first one has been done for you.

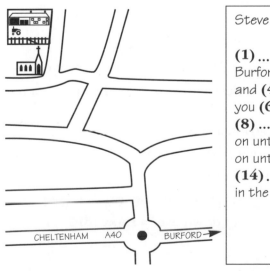

Steve

(1) ....Take...... the A40 out of Cheltenham and **(2)** .... the signs to Burford. Just before you get into Burford, **(3)** .... left at the roundabout and **(4)** .... on until you **(5)** .... to a fork in the road, where you **(6)** .... left. **(7)** .... going for another half a mile and **(8)** .... the first **(9)** .... on your right. Go **(10)** .... on until you **(11)** .... a crossroads. Turn **(12)** .... and carry on until you **(13)** .... a church. Turn right and our farm is **(14)** .... your left, just **(15)** .... the church. You'll see my car in the drive.

See you Saturday.

Pat

4.1 Wordcheck – The body and physical well-being

Complete the crossword below. The first letter of each word has been provided and one down has been done for you.

Across

2 A strong pain caused by a muscle suddenly tightening. (5)

3 A physical condition or mental illness that severely affects your life. (10)

7 To protect your skin against ultra violet light wear a good sun .... (6)

9 Salt .... is another way of saying a lack of salt. (10).

10 The ability to keep going over a long period of time. (7)

12 A part of your body where two bones meet. (5)

13 If a condition is ...., it is very severe or intense. (5)

14 An exercise in which you jump up and down over a rope. (8)

Down

1 The movement of blood through your body. (11)

3 Overexposure to the sun can cause .... to the skin. (6)

4 All the actions taken to make a sick or injured person well again. (9)

5 A home-made .... for a cold is hot lemon juice with honey. (6)

6 Ways of making people better – usually without drugs or operations e.g. hydro .... for people with arthritis. (7)

8 A synonym for illness. (7)

11 An example of **7 down** – frequently used for people with back problems. (7)

4.2 Pronunciation

The following parts of the body all contain silent letters. Cross out the silent letter(s) in each case. Look at the example given.

1 thigh	4 wrist	7 calf
2 knee	5 muscle	8 knuckles
3 thumb	6 wrinkles	9 stomach

Unit 14

1.1 ...ing or infinitive?

Match up the beginnings and endings of the following sentences and add a suitable verb either with *-ing* or in the infinitive. Look at the example.

1 The train had to stop suddenly [E]

2 I'd been calling our dog for ages ☐

3 Poor Alison absolutely dreads .... ☐

4 I remember .... it in a safe place ☐

5 I meant .... you a ring to tell you I'd be late ☐

6 Polly tried .... happy and relaxed ☐

7 British Rail regrets .... passengers ☐

8 Why don't you try .... the car – ☐

9 The doctor forgot .... me how often ☐

10 After a few weeks working with Gwendoline ☐

11 Will you remember .... the gas bill ☐

12 I dread .... what would have happened ☐

13 Victor really regrets .... university ☐

14 I'll never forget .... mistaken ☐

A I had to take the tablets.

B or had I better do it myself?

C but everyone could see she'd been crying.

D but I just didn't have the time.

E to avoid ......crashing......into a cow lying on the tracks!

F for a famous actor when I arrived at Madrid airport.

G if the lifeguard hadn't seen you.

H that all trains are subject to delay due to the snow.

I I came .... what an extraordinary person she was.

J before he came .... out of the wood with a rabbit in his mouth.

K but I've no idea where!

L before completing his degree.

M that might get it started?

N and has to take half a bottle of tranquillisers before she'll set foot on a plane.

STUDY TIP ► -ing or infinitive

- With the verbs *remember, forget, regret* and *stop* the choice between *-ing* or the infinitive depends on whether the verb following them happens **before** or **after**.
  -ing = before
  infinitive = after

e.g. Do you remember meeting me last year?
meeting happened **before** *remember*

Did you remember to post that letter?
to post happened (or not) **after** *remember*

1.2   ...ing forms, infinitive with or without 'to'

In the following sentences, circle the correct form of the verbs in bold. The first one is shown as an example.

1 I'd rather not **to/go/going** very far in the new car until I've got used **to/drive/driving** it.

2 Max dreads **to/be/being** made redundant as he's too old **to/get/getting** another decent job.

3 I spent all afternoon **to/listen/listening** to the neighbours **to/argue/arguing** about whose turn it was to mow the lawn!

4 I noticed the girl **to/put/putting** the watch into her pocket without **to/pay/paying** for it.

5 Hadn't you better **to/start/starting to/revise/revising** for the exam?

6 I think Rodney rather resents Jessica **to/participate/participating** in the conference.

7 The fire brigade had **to/be/being** called **to/get/getting** the boys down from the roof.

8 Why not **to/go/going** by train rather than **to/take/taking** the car?

9 Louise has always hated her father **to/tell/telling** her what to do.

10 The council was **to/ban/banning** all parking in the city centre but there were so many complaints they've decided not to.

11 I didn't dare **to/show/showing** them the damage I'd done to their car.

12 We're bound **to/run/running** out of cash so don't forget **to/bring/bringing** your credit card.

13 If this is a private matter, perhaps you'd prefer me **to/leave/leaving**.

14 Our physical education teacher used **to/make/making** us **to/go/going** swimming in an outdoor pool even in winter!

STUDY TIP ▶ see/hear etc. someone + do/doing

- Remember that when these verbs are followed by the *-ing* form we are talking about only part of the action not the complete action:

e.g. We watched the boys playing cricket. (we didn't see the whole game)

- When they are followed by the infinitive (without *to*) we are talking about the complete action:

e.g. We watched the boys take the equipment back to the pavilion.

2 *Review of tenses*

In the following passage, put the verbs in brackets into a suitable (active or passive) tense and put any adverbial expressions in the correct place. The first one has been done for you.

It pays to listen to the news

I must admit that Maria's English **(1)** ......*is improving*........ (improve) every day. Three weeks ago she **(2)** .... (manage) to book us on to the Portsmouth to Santander ferry at the local travel agent's.

The night before we **(3)**.............................(be) due to leave, she **(4)**.............................(ring) me up to remind me to be on time.

'Don't forget the train **(5)** .... (leave) at 7.35 and if we **(6)** .... (miss) that, we **(7)** .... (miss) the ferry too!' she said.

'Of course I **(8)** .... (get) there on time,' I replied, somewhat annoyed. 'You're the one who **(9)** ....(always turn up) late for things!'

Surprisingly, we both **(10)** .... (arrive) at the station in time **(11)**.............................. (catch) the train. We **(12)** .... (sit) on the train for about ten minutes when we realised, to our horror, that it **(13)** ....(go) in the wrong direction! We got off at the next station where a ticket seller informed us that there **(14)** .... (not be) another train to Portsmouth until 8.45. We explained that we had to catch the ferry at 10 o'clock.

'Well, if I **(15)** .... (be) you,' he said, 'I **(16)** .... (catch) the coach. That should get you to Portsmouth before the ferry **(17)** ....(sail). But you **(18)** ....(have) to hurry, it **(19)** ....(leave) the bus station in about five minutes!'

We shot off like lightning despite the heavy rucksacks on our backs and jumped on the coach just as the driver **(20)** .... (shut) the doors. We **(21)** .... (just collapse) in our seats with a sigh of relief, when the driver announced, 'Sorry everyone but the motorway **(22)** .... (still repair) so we **(23)** ....(not get) to Portsmouth until 9.45.'

We groaned in despair. That gave us only fifteen minutes to get to the ferry terminal.

We arrived at Portsmouth bus station at 9.40 and jumped straight into a taxi.

'The Santander ferry terminal and please hurry,' I shouted, 'or it **(24)** .... (go) before we **(25)**.............................. (get) there!'

To our astonishment, the taxi driver calmly switched off the engine and turned round.

'**(26)** .... you .... (not hear)?' he said, smiling, 'the ferry workers **(27)** .... (come) out on strike last night!'

'Oh no!' I cried in disbelief. 'If only I **(28)**.............................. (listen) to the news this morning!'

3 Editing skills

In most lines of the following text there is one word which is wrongly spelled, including the use of capital letters. Underline each wrongly spelled word and write the correct spelling in the space provided. If there are no spelling mistakes in a line, indicate this with a tick (✔). Look at the examples provided.

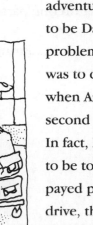

If you're going skiing this winter, here's a cautionary tale.
1 ....✔.......

Last december three friends decided to go on a cheap skiing
2 ..December..

holiday in the dolomites in the north of Italy. Being an
3 ....

adventureous lot, they decided to go by car, which turned out
4 ....

to be Dan's ancient VW Beetle. On the way there, they had no
5 ....

problems except for a little quarreling about whose turn it
6 ....

was to drive. The trouble started on there first day's skiing
7 ....

when Amy paniced, fell over and broke her ankle. On the
8 ....

second day, Charlie woke up saying, 'I think I'm dieing'.
9 ....

In fact, he had caught pneumonia. On the third day, Dan tryed
10 ....

to be too clever and broke a leg! All of this meant they
11 ....

payed plenty in doctors' bills and then, with nobody able to
12 ....

drive, they traveled back by plane and the car went back by
13 ....

train! So, all in all, it was an extremly expensive trip!
14 ....

4 Wordcheck – Studying and examinations

In the grid below there are **18** words connected with studying and taking exams. **7** are hidden horizontally, **7** vertically and **4** diagonally. When you have found them all, complete the sentences with some of them. Three have been found for you.

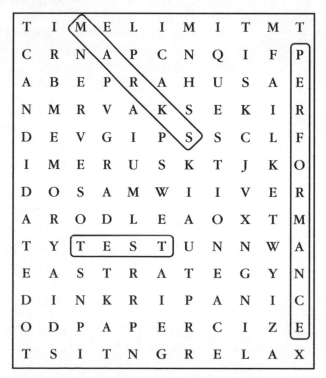

1 A student who enters for an exam is called a ....

2 It's a good idea to try and use some .... aids when preparing for the exam.

3 Another verb meaning to *take* an examination is ....

4 Stretching and breathing exercises can help you keep your exam .... under control.

5 Read all the .... carefully before attempting to answer them and .... all your answers before the end of the exam.

6 Most people try not only to .... the exam but also to get a good ....

7 Be careful not to spend too long on one part of the exam; remember there is a ....

8 Stay calm and try not to .... during the exam as this can badly affect your ....

Progress Test Four

Units 12 – 14

Check your progress by entering your score in the box at the end of each exercise and at the end of the complete test.

1 Complete the following passage by writing a word or words in each of the numbered gaps.

Business affairs

Jeff Weaver knew it was going to be a tough meeting. A year ago he **(1)** .... regarded as the company's rising star in the export department, signing contracts for massive orders from state-run companies in Lavania. It looked **(2)**........................ he had saved the company's fortunes. But all that was before the collapse of the Lavanian economy and the inevitable non-payment of most invoices.

The Managing Director, Derek Robinson, had decided to **(3)** .... an extraordinary meeting **(4)** ....into the matter. Jeff was now about **(5)** .... asked to give a detailed explanation of the disaster.

Mr Robinson coughed and tapped the table. 'Right then, everyone. Let's get **(6)**........................ business. I'm sure you're all aware of the reasons for this meeting. So without further preamble, I'll call on Mr Weaver who, I hope, will **(7)** ....to put our minds at **(8)** .... about this worrying state of affairs.'

Jeff stood up and decided to go on the attack. 'Thank you, Mr Robinson. First of all, I must admit that many mistakes **(9)**........................ over the past twelve months – but not just by me! I think it's clear that I **(10)**........................ used as a shield to protect a number of more senior colleagues, who **(11)**........................ have the courage to assume some responsibility for this mess. In particular, my immediate superior, Georgina Bunyon, who has never seen **(12)** .... eye with me, and who is using this crisis **(13)**........................ a way of **(14)**........................ me removed from the company!'

Everyone turned to look at Georgina, who **(15)** .... her fists and glaring pointedly at Jeff.

'No one **(16)**........................predicted the collapse of the Lavanian economy. However, **(17)**........................ further embarrassment, I have decided to resign.' And with this, Jeff marched out of the meeting.

Two months later, Jeff and Georgina were sitting looking at Lake Como from the terrace of a beautiful villa **(18)** .... they had just bought with part of what they called their 'Lavanian fund'.

'Any regrets, darling?' asked Georgina.

'Only one,' said Jeff smiling. 'I wish we **(19)** ....twice as much! And you?'

'Well, I **(20)** .... loved to see old Robinson's face when he found out what had happened to all that money!'

20

93

2 Fill each blank with a suitable form of the word in brackets.

Example: Your *performance* (perform) in exams is greatly influenced by your state of mind.

1 I'm terribly sorry. Did I .... (pronounce) your name?

2 Resting your back for very long periods after a serious injury may eventually lead to chronic .... (able).

3 Apparently, we .... (memory) things through association.

4 If you get cramp in your calf, ... (straight) your knee and pull your foot backwards.

5 A thorough .... (know) of local customs and etiquette can be vital to a businessman.

6 One thing examiners can't stand in exam scripts is bad .... (write).

7 The basic idea of good manners is to avoid a feeling of .... (embarrass).

8 Shaking hands is the .... (custom) way of greeting business counterparts in Europe.

9 Stretching your back is a good way of relieving .... (stiff).

10 Americans' attempts to be friendly and informal may be taken as a sign of .... (respect) in more formal societies.

10

3 Complete each of the following sentences with the appropriate form of a suitable phrasal verb. An example is shown.

Example: We all thought the lecture would be rather boring but it *turned out* to be extremely interesting.

1 As we didn't have an instructions manual, we had to .... how to set up the stereo by trial and error.

2 It's a formal occasion so we'll have to get .... to the nines – no jeans and pullovers this time!

3 Toby's .... really well at his new job. He's already been promoted twice.

4 Sarah's really lucky. She left her car in a no-parking area for eight hours and, believe it or not, she .... with it!

5 Oh dear, Helen, your glass is almost empty. Let me..............lt .... for you.

5

4 In most lines of the following text there is one unnecessary word. It is either grammatically incorrect or does not fit in with the sense of the text. For each numbered line, find the unnecessary word and then write it in the space provided. Some lines are correct. Indicate these with a tick (✔). The first two lines have been done for you.

Obsessive note-taking which is the occupational hazard of	**e.g.**	*which*
students. They believe they remember things best by writing them	**e.g.**	✔
down. Writing things down, however, is a practice that it can	**1**	....
be abused as it can so easily lead back to a passive and	**2**	....
unconfident attitude to books. Every little point the student	**3**	....
reads may, in its context, be so persuasive and that he feels	**4**	....
obliged to include it in his notes. These tend become an abridged	**5**	....
version of the original. What the obsessive note-taker usually	**6**	....
postpones learning by understanding till he comes to read in his	**7**	....
notes; but as such these are not always the product of	**8**	....
understanding they may be lengthy and unreliable. Furthermore,	**9**	....
sentence-by-sentence or paragraph-by-paragraph note-taking	**10**	....
which commits the reader to further page-by-page reading; and as	**11**	....
we shall see later, this situation is not necessarily the best	**12**	....
way of reading slowly and understanding a book. The reader's	**13**	....
notes should be both the outcome of understanding and not	**14**	....
the prelude to it. Notes written of this kind are brief.	**15**	....

15

TOTAL

50

Answer Key

Unit 1

1.1

2 yes 3 no 4 yes 5 yes 6 no 7 no 8 no 9 yes 10 yes

1.2

2 taken back/brought back/returned 3 cooked in
4 given/treated with 5 left/allowed 6 booked by/reserved by
7 taken/stolen/ removed/parked/left in 8 dug up at (on)/
found at (on)/discovered at (on)/unearthed at (on)
9 washed in/with 10 painted 11 brought into/
imported into 12 left

2

2 on … stand-by 3 warned … against 4 admission of
5 under … illusions 6 cleared of 7 into action 8 increase
in 9 on … route 10 fitted with

3

2 ground 3 laid 4 bitten 5 dealt 6 struck 7 frozen
8 ridden 9 dug 10 wound 11 stung 12 hidden 13 shown
14 spread 15 rose 16 shrunk

4 (corrected verbs only)

2 swimming 4 dying 5 kidnapped 7 paid 8 tried
9 arguing 10 referred 11 played 12 panicked

5 (model answer)

> 10 North Parade
> Loxley
>
> 15 April, 19—
>
> The Chairman
> Town Council
> Loxley
>
> Dear Sir,
>
> I am writing to express my concern about the appalling state of the road outside my house. Indeed, the road is in such bad repair that my nextdoor neighbour recently had the misfortune to get the back wheel of her car stuck in one of the enormous pot-holes outside my gate. She was not only most distressed by the incident but also had to pay for a breakdown truck to pull her car out.
>
> The damage to the road surface is clearly the result of the period of extremely cold weather we had with ice and snow. That, however, was two months ago now and still nothing has been done, despite the fact that the road was inspected by a member of the council immediately after the weather improved.
>
> I must, therefore, insist that the council takes steps to have the road repaired as soon as possible. Moreover, I must urge the council to take appropriate action to ensure that situations like this are rectified more promptly in the future.
>
> I look forward to hearing from you.
>
> Yours faithfully,
>
> *Fred Smith*
>
> Fred Smith

6.1

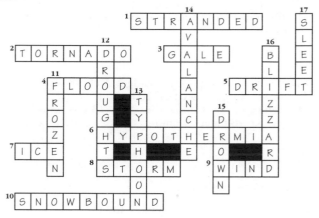

6.2

2 I 3 H 4 F 5 J 6 A 7 C 8 G 9 B 10 D

Unit 2

1.1

2 OK 3 Isn't that the hotel Greg and Sally had their wedding reception in? 4 The gentleman you spoke to last time is no longer with the company. 5 OK 6 OK
7 The reason the accident happened has never been clarified. 8 Is this the picture you were referring to? 9 OK
10 That's the car we were thinking of buying.

1.2

1b whose mayor was arrested for corruption? c which/that was completely destroyed during the war? d where Richard Burton was born? 2a whose author I can never remember the name of? b which/that was reviewed in the Times last week? c (which/that) I lent you last term? 3a who lived in China until she was 16? b (who/that) the restaurant sacked for being rude to customers? c whose boyfriend wants to go and live in Italy? 4a (which/that) you wanted to have off?
b which/that had to be invented to make the year longer?
c when most people get married?

2.1

2 as soon as/when/once 3 until 4 after 5 while 6 if
7 when/once/as soon as 8 until 9 by the time
10 once/when/as soon as

2.2 (suggested answers only)

2 you've finished 3 you're seeing the bank manager
4 we get there 5 've finished the exam 6 you leave the car here 7 go to bed 8 has worn off

3

2 're forever using 3 know 4 's going 5 leaves 6 's writing
7 always gives 8 doesn't seem, 's always leaving
9 're having 10 rescues, gets 11 are you living
12 serves, returns, goes

4

2 B how much 3 H which 4 A what 5 how C 6 when I
7 what E 8 J how 9 G who 10 D whose

5

2 pronoun 3 base form 4 adjective 5 article 6 auxiliary
verb 7 preposition 8 participle 9 conjunction 10 adverb
11 pronoun 12 -ing noun 13 noun 14 modal 15 article
16 adverb

6

1 chatting 2 interruptions 4 gadget 5 chess 6 crossword
7 counters 8 jigsaw 9 clues 10 lawnmower
11 brainteaser 12 window-shopping 13 gossiping
Hidden word: timeconsuming

Unit 3

1 (suggested answers only)

2 Driving carelessly 3 Listening to the radio 4 Watching TV
5 Living abroad 6 Doing 7 Swimming 8 Reading
9 Having a bath 10 Biting your nails

2

2 of going 3 of stealing 4 about accepting 5 in doing
6 at taking 7 about seeing 8 for inviting 9 in going
10 of seeing 11 for breaking 12 for forgetting 13 of telling
14 by pressing 15 after coming 16 for getting
17 when/while operating/using 18 before overtaking

3

2 drinking 3 seeing 4 to cut 5 working, having
6 to realise 7 telling 8 to tell 9 to win 10 relying/
depending, to stand 11 to pass, playing 12 wondering,
coming/getting 13 smoking, breathing 14 to take,
fixing/repairing/adjusting 15 promising, to help, getting

4

2 showing 3 following 4 sightings 5 airing 6 reading
7 saying 8 carving 9 setting 10 awakening 11 hearing
12 recording 13 beings 14 fittings 15 spellings

5

2 K 3 J 4 A/O 5 H 6 L 7 E 8 M 9 D 10 N 11 B 12 C
13 O/A 14 F 15 I

6

2 C result 3 H caused 4 K result 5 D effect
6 F source/cause 7 L cause 8 E result 9 A result
10 G because 11 J lead 12 B due

7.1

2 rush (the others are connected with sleeping) 3 wriggle
(the others are connected with holding something)
4 symptom (is not an example of a specific physical problem)

5 unwind (the others are ways of avoiding stress or illness)
6 arteries (the others are external parts of the body – legs
and feet) 7 vulnerable (the other adjectives describe
frequent reactions to stress) 8 stroke (the other verbs are
connected with breathing)

7.2

2 E 3 H 4 G 5 A 6 D 7 F 8 B

Unit 4

1 (suggested answers only)

2 broke down/ran out of petrol 3 you work 4 (should) see
him 5 will we get to 6 I have 7 I'd slap 8 you use it/you
look after it 9 I spoke/could speak 10 you require (any)
11 wouldn't get/have 12 you were shipwrecked/stranded
13 I were/was 14 it rains 15 didn't (always) have

2

2 OK 3 strange round Persian 4 extraordinary large orange
straw 5 amazing tiny new 6 OK 7 big red American 8 OK
9 incredibly popular little Italian 10 lovely big round

3 (model answers)

2 Present continuous – I'm working in Dublin this month.
3 Present perfect simple – I've already eaten so I'm not
hungry, thanks.
4 Present perfect continuous – **a** I've been waiting for an
hour. **b** I've been sunbathing in the garden; that's why my
face is so red.
5 Past continuous – **a** I was picking grapes in France this
time last week. **b** I was de-frosting the fridge when the
phone rang.
6 Past perfect simple – By the time the police arrived, the
robbers had already escaped.
7 Past perfect continuous – I had been working for ten
hours when I fell asleep exhausted.
8 Future continuous – I'll be relaxing at the seaside this
time next month.
9 Future perfect simple – I hope I'll have read her book
when I meet her next week.
10 Future perfect continuous – I'll have been working here
for three years next June.

4 (suggested answers only)

2 carefully, now 3 the most expensive, the worst
4 but, moreover 5 hers, mine 6 information, luggage
7 bigger, more interesting 8 tall, funny 9 never, nobody
10 was kidnapped, were arrested

5

2 underrate, overrate 3 understatement, overstatement
4 undernourished 5 undercharge, overcharge
6 understaffed, overstaffed

6 (model answer)

> ### Report on the new 'Bambo' pushchair
>
> **Introduction**
> The aim of this report is to find out how good the new 'Bambo' pushchair is. It is based on interviews with 150 mothers and fathers in six different cities all over Britain.
>
> **Observations and comments**
> It was found that the majority of people interviewed had a very favourable overall impression of the pushchair. In the words of a Mrs Long of Gloucester, comparing it with her old pushchair, '*The 'Bambo' is fantastic – it's so light and manageable*', and as a Mr Blair of London said, it must be comfortable as his little boy '*really likes going out in it*'. On the whole, most people interviewed agree the 'Bambo' has the following good points: it is light and easy to steer; it is good for carrying shopping on the tray under the baby's seat; it is colourful and attractive to look at; the baby seems comfortable as (s)he has 4 different positions ranging from lying flat to sitting upright; it is easy to transport as it takes up very little room when folded. There were, however, some negative comments, which were: the opening hinge is often stiff making it difficult to unfold; the wheels themselves are rather small, which means the pushchair often gets stuck in holes on uneven or rough ground; the wheel locking mechanism on the back wheels is too small to be operated by using one's foot, which means one has to bend down to lock it by hand.
>
> **Recommendations**
> It is advisable for 'Bocia' to make the following changes to their current model of 'Bambo' pushchair: a) make the opening hinge easier to operate, b) increase the size of the wheels, c) make the wheel locking mechanism large enough to be operated by foot.
>
> **Conclusion**
> To sum up, the current model is already well established as one of the best pushchairs on the market. However, acting on the recommendations stated above, 'Bocia' should be able to improve the product still further and possibly become market leader.

7

Progress Test One

1 (score one point for each correct answer)

1 which 2 as 3 over 4 Having 5 going 6 spite 7 While/As
8 who 9 would/might 10 without 11 good 12 where
13 matter 14 queuing 15 until 16 apologising
17 understaffed 18 result 19 under 20 unless/although

2 (score one point for each correct answer)

1 unavoidable 2 underdone 3 enables 4 Anxiety
5 consolidate 6 responsibility 7 insecurity 8 countless
9 invaluable 10 stressful

3 (score one point for each correct answer)

1 lead to 2 ringing up/phoning up 3 weigh up
4 let … down 5 rounded off/finished off

4 (points for each fully correct answer are shown in brackets – deduct one point for every mistake)

b The four lads from Hereford/They are four lads from Hereford (who) met at university where they were studying Physics. **(2 points)**
c Their first hit, (called) 'Closed Circuit', stayed/was in the Top 10 for five weeks. **(2 points)**
d At present they are arranging a tour of Eastern Europe which starts/is planned to start/will start next month. **(2 points)**
e They also have/There is also a new album (called) 'Like Poles Repel' which is going to/due to/will be released next month. **(2 points)**
f Their ambition is to make it in the USA, where they've had no hits so far. **(2 points)**
g The lead singer, Rick Springer, says he has no girlfriend(s) because he has no time! **(2 points)**
h The others say they're fairly settled with steady girlfriends. **(1 point)**
i They'll/The group will be back from Europe next year when they'll be doing/'re going to do 15 concerts in the UK. **(2 points)**

Unit 5

1

2 was living, met 3 Weren't you working, had 4 got, became 5 heard, was going 6 went, left 7 lived, were always having 8 was hoping 9 was living, was published 10 saw, was blowing, were gathering 11 were lying, was working 12 rang, picked, put 13 never understood, always got 14 worked, went 15 was, always went, really loved, often rained

2.1

2 brush up 3 zip it up 4 do up 5 livened up 6 round up
7 brighten up 8 gang up 9 chained up 10 speed up

2.2

2 it out/away 3 after him 4 it up 5 it back 6 it up 7 to it
8 it over/about it 9 it in/out 10 it up 11 them up
12 her round

2.3

2 looked on to 3 dropped off 4 build up 5 taken aback
6 pulled up 7 stubbed out 8 go through with 9 pull out
10 started up 11 pulled over 12 jumped out of
13 shot off 14 pulled … off

3

2 will have finished 3 gets, 'll have 4 's going to fall
5 is due to open; 'll have been completed 7 is to/is due to/is going to give/is giving 8 'll be 9 doesn't start, 'll have
10 's going to have/'s having 11 'll be flying 12 'll phone

13 'll have finished 14 Shall I give, is Fred going to take/will Fred be taking/is Fred taking 15 're about to/going to close

4.1

2 steward, take-off 3 check in 4 Lavatories 5 terminal
6 boarding card 7 standby 8 delay, take off

4.2

Unit 6

1.1

2 so/as intelligent as 3 better 4 the most carefully 5 as/so mountainous a country as 6 most northern/most northerly/northernmost 7 as much time … as 8 as careful a driver as 9 more frequently than 10 the heaviest

1.2

2 C 3 F 4 J 5 H 6 E 7 K 8 I 9 D 10 L 11 A 12 B

1.3

2 as blind as a bat 3 as flat as a pancake 4 as dry as a bone 5 as fresh as a daisy 6 as slippery as an eel 7 as weak as a kitten 8 as stubborn as a mule 9 as thin as a rake 10 as proud as a peacock 11 as strong as an ox 12 as deaf as a post

2

2 Hardly had she stubbed out one cigarette when she lit another. 3 Not a soul did we see all day. 4 No sooner did/had I put the phone down than it rang again. 5 So quietly did he speak that I didn't hear a thing he said.
6 Not a (single) game did they win all season. 7 Such is life.
8 Only after she'd been speaking to him for ten minutes did she realise who he was. 9 Not only did Kate spill wine on the carpet, but she also broke six glasses.
10 Never (before) had I seen such a gigantic fish!

3

2 as 3 alike, like 4 as 5 alike 6 like 7 as 8 like

4

2 Not only, but also 3 Moreover/Furthermore
4 In addition to/As well as/Besides 5 as if/as though
6 Although/Even though/Though 7 Even if 8 yet 9 in spite

of/despite 10 However 11 nevertheless 12 whereas/while

5 Layout and style mistakes:

```
                                    1 Andy Kulmbacher
                                    2 25 Bramley Road
                                      Burnville BV2 6BZ
        3                             23rd Oct, 19—
    Dear Paco,

    4        5 It was very …
    …… see you soon.
    Looking forward to hearing from you. 6

              7 Best wishes,
```

Missing phrases:

1 hear from you 2 I was/am glad 3 I wonder (I was wondering) if I could ask/I need (want) to ask you a 4 I'd be (terribly/really/very) grateful 5 hesitate to say no/worry 6 Anyway 7 Hope to/I hope to

6

2 punctuation 3 mother tongue 4 register 5 slang
6 official language 7 context 8 script

Unit 7

1 (some variations are possible)

2 slightly older than 3 exactly half as much as 4 much more than 5 a little/slightly shorter than 6 considerably shorter than 7 three times as many hours per day as
8 slightly fewer hours per day than 9 about half as much (money) as 10 over five times as much (money) as
11 a great deal more exercise than 12 slightly less exercise than

2 (suggested answers)

2 you rather have a pizza or a curry? 3 rather you didn't bring the dog into/have the dog in the house. 4 you rather I didn't tell Anna about this? 5 you rather I'd told you I was coming to stay? 6 rather play golf than watch it on TV.
7 you rather have gone out tonight? 8 rather you didn't phone the doctor.

3

2 did you see, haven't seen 3 've known, for 4 has Nick been studying, Did he fail 5 Has Rob finished, has just been 6 've been living, since, got 7 have you had
8 've been looking, has she left 9 haven't repaired
10 hasn't won 11 Have you been doing 12 Has Maisy phoned, said 13 have you eaten 14 've been using, since, haven't found 15 has eaten/been eating, since

4

A 1 noun 2 adverb 3 adjective 4 adjective
B 5 with a lot of hair, neutral 6 dangerous, negative
7 amusing, positive 8 strange, negative
9 pleasant, positive 10 small, neutral
C 11 G 12 I 13 B 14 H 15 C 16 D 17 E 18 J
19 A 20 F
D 21 useless 22 usable 23 used 24 Users 25 usefully
E 26 buoy 27 wrestling 28 knock 29 comb 20 sword

31 guitar **32** photographer **33** difficulty **34** calculator **35** original

5

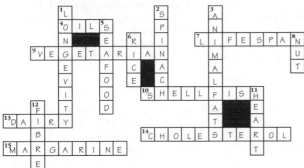

Unit 8

1

2 be able to come 3 must have taken 4 might have left 5 could/might/may have got 6 could swim 7 was able to swim 8 could/might have told 9 couldn't find 10 be able to run, can't even run 11 mightn't/can't have realised 12 can cause 13 couldn't have been 14 Can you see, might/could/may well be 15 could have been 16 can't be 17 hasn't been able to hear 18 might/may bite

2

2 (give) up 3 (turned) up 4 OK 5 turned (out) 6 (sorted) out 7 OK 8 (making) for 9 OK 10 (stick) to 11 (write) off 12 OK

3 (some variations are possible)

2 Colin promised he'd/to repair the back door last/that weekend. 3 Karen admitted she'd scratched the car. 4 Maurice threatened to tell the police if they didn't give/unless they gave him £5,000. 5 Hilary insisted that I go/went to Dave's party with her on Saturday. 6 Silvia mentioned that Terry's house was still for sale. 7 Mr Penfold swore he'd never seen the money before. 8 The mountain guide warned them not to go walking in the fog (because it could be dangerous). 9 He couldn't remember if it was Leonardo or Michelangelo who painted/had painted the Mona Lisa. 10 Julian announced/told us/informed us that he and Nina were getting married the following year. 11 Jemima boasted/claimed she was the best tennis-player at the college. 12 Dr Bianchi asked Dr McPherson if (s)he'd mind repeating the question/to repeat his/her question. 13 George complained that the service in the restaurant was incredibly slow. 14 The shop assistant suggested it might be better to/that I (should) wait until the manager got there. 15 The doctor advised Jack to eat less and take more exercise.

4 (corrected mistakes numbered and shown in bold)

> 5 Redland Road
> Barford BF2 8VR
> 21st May, 19—

Randolph Jefferies
20 The Green
Hinton
Devon HN3 2CC

Dear (1) Mr **Jefferies**

I was most interested (2) **in** your advertisement (3) **in** 'The Independent' and I am writing (4) **to** obtain further (5) **information** about your country cottage holidays.

In particular, I would like (6) **to know** in which parts of the country your cottages are located as my friends and I are interested (7) **in** staying as far away from large cities as possible. I would (8) **also** like to know if it would be possible (9) **to rent** a cottage for six people for up to six months and whether pets are allowed as my friends and I have three well-behaved dogs we are planning to take with us.

I should, therefore, be (10) **most/extremely/terribly** grateful if you (11) **would** send me full details of your larger more isolated cottages and any brochures you may have.

Thanking you in advance for your help. I look forward to (12) **hearing** from you as (13) **soon** as possible.

Yours (14) **sincerely**,
Sandy Melville

5.1

2 courier 3 self-catering 4 tip 5 postcard 6 snapshots 7 balcony 8 campsite 9 suntan 10 package 11 sightseeing 12 excursion 13 sandcastles **Hidden word:** holidaymakers

5.2

2 F 3 J 4 G 5 I 6 E 7 B 8 D 9 A 10 H

Progress Test Two

1 (score one point for each correct answer)

1 was wondering/wondered 2 turn/show 3 've been waiting 4 heavier/worse than 5 able to 6 were driving past/were going past 7 set 8 was driving/going 9 have you had 10 like 11 Can't/Couldn't 12 'll do/'m doing 13 up 14 bit/little/lot/good (great) deal 15 must have 16 were waiting 17 was/would be 18 was able/managed 19 'm not coming/won't be (coming) 20 found

2 (score one point for each correct answer)

1 eyesight 2 light-headed 3 expectancy 4 drawback 5 passers-by 6 consumption 7 broadcasts 8 guidelines 9 greenhouse 10 nowadays

3 (score one point for each correct answer)

1 turned out 2 stood by 3 handed down 4 singles out 5 stick to

4 (score one point only if you have the correct combination and the correct particle)

2 I down 3 H up 4 A up 5 F about/around 6 K up 7 J after 8 C out 9 B out 10 E up 11 D over

5 (score one point for each correct answer)

1 G 2 E 3 H 4 C 5 B

Unit 9

1

2 no commas 3 OK 4 no commas 5 OK 6 comma before *which* 7 comma before *which* 8 comma before *which* and after *chimpanzees* 9 OK 10 comma before *whose* and after *dog*

2.1

2 cut up 3 dip into 4 holding ... up 5 carrying out 6 sprung up 7 make up 8 cut down

2.2

2 cut down 3 made up 4 make up 5 held up 6 dip into 7 hold up 8 sprang up

3

2 ... both (of them) have ... 3 Neither. 4 £1 each (one). 5 ... they both lead ... 6 OK 7 OK or Every record ... 8 ... but neither of them ... 9 OK 10 OK

4

2 so that/in order that 3 in case 4 due to/owing to/as a result of/because of 5 As/Since/Because 6 so ... that 7 so 8 such ... that 9 consequently/therefore/as a result 10 As soon as/When/Once 11 until/till 12 Before 13 Hardly ... when or No sooner ... than 14 First, Then/Next/After that, Finally 15 While

5

A 2 immobile 3 irrational 4 uncomfortable 5 non-smoker 6 irrelevant 7 unreliable 8 disrespect 9 insoluble 10 misbehave 11 illogical 12 discomfort 13 misspell 14 impolite 15 illegible 16 non-resident

B 17 rude – polite 18 clever/intelligent – stupid/unintelligent 19 thin – plump/fat 20 useful/convenient – useless/inconvenient

6

2 166 High Street 3 in applying 4 post/position of 5 was advertised/I saw advertised 6 My reason for 7 have worked/been working 8 interested in/looking for 9 offer/give me 10 of working 11 to attend an 12 convenient 13 I look forward to hearing from you 14 Yours sincerely, 15 OLIVIA JAMES

7

2 fuels 3 recycling 4 drought 5 timber 6 bleach 7 packaging 8 greenhouse

Unit 10

1

2 turned up 3 explained 4 had been held up 5 didn't find 6 had been blowing 7 (had) called 8 was lying 9 had been driving 10 (had) appeared 11 (had) braked 12 (had) skidded 13 (had) managed 14 was filling up

15 was wearing 16 had tied 17 was pulling 18 opened 19 jumped 20 had swum

2.1

2 would still be living, hadn't found 3 hadn't looked, wouldn't have spotted 4 would ever have guessed, hadn't been caught 5 would never have got, hadn't been/gone 6 had taken, might/would be living 7 hadn't noticed, would be 8 would have been, hadn't lost 9 wouldn't be, hadn't known 10 'd listened, wouldn't be sitting

2.2

2 If we hadn't got soaking wet on Sunday, we wouldn't (all) have colds (now). 3 If I knew, I'd tell you. 4 We'll have to cancel the barbecue if the weather's bad on Saturday. 5 I wouldn't be living in Italy if I hadn't got married to an Italian. 6 I would have phoned you if I hadn't lost the bit of paper with your number on. 7 If she weren't/wasn't so aggressive, we'd get on (much better). 8 We wouldn't have a broken window if you and your friends hadn't been playing football in the back yard. 9 If I hadn't missed the end of the film, I'd know who the murderer was. 10 If Jimmie passes his exams, his father will/is going to buy him a new bike. 11 We'd have gone to the cinema if we hadn't already seen the film. 12 Zoe would have won the race if she hadn't tripped and fallen.

3.1

2 put ... down to 3 brought out 4 cut off 5 put out 6 get over 7 broke out 8 cut off

3.2

2 got over 3 put ... down to 4 cut ... off 5 got over 6 broke out 7 put out 8 brings ... out

4 (model answer)

. . . then find the opening for the cartridge in the back of the printer. Don't forget to make sure there's nothing inside the opening! Once you've done that, put the cartridge in the hole with the socket facing you. Then just slide it in but be careful not to force it. When you hear a click, you know it's in OK. Next do up the screw nice and tight. Finally plug in the cable from the computer and away you go!

5

Unit 11

1.1

2 is spread/put F 3 was invented D 4 will be/will have been wiped out/eradicated L 5 used to be/were extracted/taken out/pulled out J 6 could be bought/ obtained I 7 should not be exposed B 8 was/used to be spoken C 9 has been/is simplified K 10 are used A 11 are being destroyed E 12 are regarded H

1.2

2 will probably be sent 3 will be/are taken 4 have already been picked 5 be picked 6 were sprayed 7 to be gathered 8 are harvested 9 are both made 10 to be made 11 is treated 12 are just shaken 13 is collected 14 (is) put 15 will be automated

2 (* = suggested answer only)

2 more/less interesting, more/less likely 3 less easy/easier, more/less highly 4 more wine, less clearly 5 closer, *more nervous 6 more humid, *worse 7 farther/further, *thicker 8 *The harder something is to do 9 *the less they practice their English 10 *The more stressful the situation

3

2 tick … off 3 put down 4 face up to 5 worked out 6 steer away from 7 eked out 8 fight … out 9 fall back on 10 picking out

4 (suggested answers only)

2 to die. 3 play on the grass. 4 to have more accidents. 5 realise how bad the situation really was. 6 to give up smoking. 7 to open his suitcase. 8 leave the room. 9 to learn to speak the language. 10 lose my temper.

5

2 I was/am glad to hear you had a good time – apart from the sunburn!
3 I hope you've got over it and are feeling better (by) now.
4 Anyway, the reason (why) I'm writing is that Kim and I are having a party on Saturday 19th to celebrate the end of our exams.
5 I know it's rather a long way (for you) to come but I was wondering if/whether you'd like to stay the whole weekend.
6 We both hope you'll be able to make it.
7 Can you let me know if you're coming (or not) by next Friday?
8 Hope to hear from you soon.

6

2 restless (the others describe someone with a strong desire to do something) 3 impatient (the others describe someone who is not aware of or doesn't care about other people's feelings) 4 diligent (the others describe someone who communicates well with other people) 5 calm (the others describe someone who finds it difficult to talk to other people) 6 carefree (the others describe someone who concentrates so as not to make mistakes) 7 charming (the others describe someone who feels/is feeling pleasure) 8 dynamic (the others describe someone you can place your faith in or trust)

Progress Test Three

1 (score one point for each correct answer)

1 who 2 persuaded/convinced 3 had been getting/becoming/growing 4 when 5 make 6 have been/are covered/hidden 7 'd know 8 until 9 which 10 had been abandoned/left/deserted 11 tougher/harder/ rougher/more difficult 12 causing 13 while 14 to make/build/start 15 After 16 to have been/be 17 meantime/meanwhile 18 No sooner 19 to repair 20 would have spent/had

2 (score one point for each correct answer)

1 workaholic 3 Discontented 3 surroundings 4 disapproval 5 outlook 6 miraculous 7 appliances 8 unappetising 9 uncommitted 10 plantations

3 (score one point for each correct answer)

1 carries out 2 gone out 3 broke out 4 send off 5 cut off

4 (score one point for each correct answer)

1 have been hung/are being hung 2 have calmed 3 contains 4 hunt 5 makes the elks avoid 6 OK 7 adding 8 OK 9 will be cut 10 costs 11 OK 12 was invented 13 stop elks eating 14 OK 15 would soon become

Unit 12

1

2 may leave 3 didn't have to change 4 needn't have rushed 5 must have/have to have/need to have 6 can/could/may/ might I ask 7 will be allowed/able to travel 8 should/ought to/must have 9 'll have to ask 10 don't have (need) to do/needn't do 11 to be allowed/able to build, can't put 12 Need we discuss/Do we need to discuss 13 should have kept 14 'll be allowed/able to build 15 weren't allowed to/couldn't make, had to use

2

2 promise 3 hold 4 experience 5 jokes 6 does 7 question/point 8 give 9 ease 10 date 11 priority 12 pay 13 made 14 blunder 15 move

3

A 1 /ʌ/ 2 /ɔː/ 3 /ɪ/ 4 /æ/ 5 /ɒ/ 6 /ɜː/ 7 /uː/ 8 /ɑː/
B 9 D 10 S 11 S 12 D 13 D 14 D 15 S 16 D 17 S 18 D
C

/ʌf/	/ə/	/aʊ/	/əʊ/	/ɔː/	/ɒf/
rough	thorough	bough	though	thought	trough
enough	borough	drought	dough	nought	cough
tough		plough			

/uː/
through

4 * = beginning of new paragraph

LETTER A: e (respond/reply, appeared/was published), * g (out), i (seems/appears, both), b (persuade). Yours faithfully,
LETTER B: k (apologise), d (due), j, (answer provided), * f (extremely/terribly/very, wasted), h (assure), * c (earliest). Yours sincerely,

5

2 embrace 3 bow 4 awkward 5 rudeness 6 impression
7 apology 8 disrespect 9 hospitality 10 compliment
11 offend 12 manners 13 conduct **Hidden word:**
embarrassment

Unit 13

1 (suggested answers only)

2 didn't interrupt me when I'm speaking. 3 left for the
station. 4 hadn't lost my temper (this morning). 5 you hadn't/
haven't seen her? 6 lost your job, what would you do then?
7 hadn't given my phone number to that insurance agent.
8 were poor/broke/didn't have any money! 9 didn't have to go
to work tomorrow. 10 hadn't held on to my belt, I'd have
fallen overboard. 11 were rich, I'd travel round the world in
my own plane. 12 called (you) back later/at another time?

2

A 2 OK 3 shrugged his sholders 4 clapping my hands
   5 stamps his feet 6 OK 7 nodded their heads 8 OK
B 9 nail B 10 foot I 11 D heart 12 hand J 13 A teeth
   14 E heels 15 H thumbs 16 C teeth 17 G eye 18 F ears

3

2 follow 3 turn 4 carry/go 5 come/get 6 bear/branch
7 Keep 8 take 9 turning/road 10 straight 11 reach
12 left 13 reach/see 14 on 15 past

4.1

4.2

2 knee 3 thumb 4 wrist 5 muscle 6 wrinkles 7 calf
8 knuckles 9 stomach

Unit 14

1.1

2 J running/walking/wandering 3 flying N 4 putting/hiding K
5 to give D 6 to look/appear C 7 to inform H 8 pushing/
kicking/shaking/hitting M 9 to tell A 10 I to realise/
understand 11 to pay B 12 to think G 13 leaving/
dropping out of L 14 being/getting F

1.2

2 being, to get 3 listening, arguing 4 put, paying 5 start
revising/to revise 6 participating 7 to be, to get 8 go,
taking 9 telling 10 to ban 11 (to) show 12 to run, to
bring 13 to leave 14 to make, go

2

2 managed 3 were 4 rang 5 leaves 6 miss 7 'll miss
8 'll get 9 's always turning/always turns up 10 arrived
11 to catch 12 had been sitting 13 was going 14 wouldn't
be/wasn't 15 were/was 16 'd catch 17 sails 18 'll have
19 leaves/'ll be leaving 20 was shutting/was going to
shut/was about to shut 21 had just collapsed 22 is still
being repaired 23 won't get/won't be getting/aren't going
to get 24 'll have gone/'ll go 25 get 26 Haven't you heard
27 came 28 'd listened

3

3 Dolomites 4 adventurous 5 OK 6 quarrelling 7 their
8 panicked 9 dying 10 tried 11 OK 12 paid 13 OK in
American English or travelled 14 extremely

4

T	I	M	E	L	I	M	I	T	M	T

(word search grid)

1 candidate
2 memory
3 sit
4 nerves
5 questions, check
6 pass, grade/mark
7 time limit
8 panic,
  performance

Progress Test Four

1 (score one point for each correct answer)

1 had been/was 2 as though/if 3 hold/call 4 to look 5 to be
6 down to/on with 7 be able/manage 8 ease/rest 9 have
been made 10 am being/have been 11 ought to/should
12 eye to 13 as 14 having/getting 15 was clenching/shaking
16 could/would have 17 to/in order to/so as to avoid 18
which/that 19 had taken/stolen 20 would have

2 (score one point for each correct answer)

1 mispronounce 2 disability 3 memorise 4 straighten
5 knowledge 6 handwriting 7 embarrassment
8 customary 9 stiffness 10 disrespect

3 (score one point for each correct answer)

1 work out 2 dressed up 3 getting on 4 got away
5 top/fill … up

4 (score one point for each correct answer)

1 it 2 back 3 OK 4 and 5 tend 6 What 7 in 8 such 9 OK
10 OK 11 which 12 situation 13 slowly 14 both
15 written